Nancy Ridley

NANCY RIDLEY'S
LOVE AFFAIR WITH HISTORY

Also by
NANCY RIDLEY

Portrait of Northumberland
Northumbrian Heritage
A Northumbrian Remembers
A Northumbrian at Large
Northumberland Then and Now

NANCY RIDLEY'S LOVE AFFAIR WITH HISTORY

by
Nancy Ridley

ORIEL PRESS
STOCKSFIELD

BOSTON   HENLEY   LONDON

© Nancy Ridley

First published in 1982
by Oriel Press Ltd (Routledge & Kegan Paul)
Branch End, Stocksfield,
Northumberland, NE43 7NA

Set in Plantin
Printed in Great Britain
by Knight & Forster, Leeds

ISBN 0 85362 191 8

FOR
LILIAN

FOREWORD

It is a great privilege to be asked to provide a foreword to a work by Nancy Ridley. Amongst present-day writers there are not many who can match her great gift of illuminating history, particularly that of our own North Country, with such pleasing and graphic style.

Those of us whose roots are in Northumberland and the Border have a rich store of history upon which to draw. She holds the key which unlocks the door for us and loosens 'the mystic chords of memory, stretching from every battlefield and patriot grave to every living heart'.

To all this, Miss Ridley has added memories of her own childhood and given us a glimpse of some of her travels, which will strike a note of sympathy in the heart of anyone who loves the countryside and especially the solitude of moor, lough and mountain.

Marson of Lindisfarne

Westminster
August 1981.

CONTENTS

CHAPTER ONE

THE EARLY YEARS

ON A SUMMER evening a long time ago, a small girl named Nancy Ridley was lifted onto the back of a horse called Scottie. The coming of Scottie to Lipwood Well, had he but known it, instigated Nancy Ridley's lifelong interest in history, especially the abortive Jacobite rebellions and the men and women involved in them.

The picture is vivid still, a green cushion brought from the kitchen was my saddle and Daddy, as I called him then, told me that Scottie had come from The Riddings, a house which was beside the river Border Esk, where a Prince whose name was Charles Edward Stuart had crossed with an army into England nearly two hundred years before. My questions were endless. Why had he come? Where did he go? What did he look like? The inquisition must have worn my father's patience to such an extent that he there and then promised that he would take me to some of the places associated with Charlie in the neighbouring county of Cumberland (now Cumbria). Take me my father did, enjoying playing Jacobites as much as I. To The Riddings we went where on the retreat from Derby,

> The Esk was swollen sae red, sae deep,
> And shouther to shouther the braw lads keep.

From the Riddings to Carlisle, into the Crown and Mitre where we saw the medallion of Charlie; home by Brampton to see the house where he spent three weeks. I am delighted to say that the house has been preserved, I was there not long ago. Little did I think that in the years to come I would follow Charlie 'over the sea to Skye', to Eriskay where he landed, to Loch Boisdale on South Uist, see the memorial to Flora Macdonald and visit the saddest battlefield in Scotland, Culloden.

Animals have played an important part in leading me to

1

people and places. A horse started my affair with Charlie, sheep dogs were my companions in early life, the poor creatures submitting to my dressing them up as historical characters! Sweep, our collie, often played the part of Flora Macdonald and had to be disrobed before he could round up the sheep.

The cat sitting beside me as I write, now a venerable old gentleman of seventeen, is an ever-present reminder of my luncheon with a Prime Minister. Tory of course; not that anyone would ever guess my politics who knows that my cat's name is Alexander Collingwood Douglas-Home Ridley! Alec for short. My love of racing and horses resulted in a friendship which I treasure, that of a brave and gallant gentleman, Clive Straker, and his famous old chaser Clybeg.

At the height of my Jacobite fever cats and teddy bears were all re-christened with appropriate historical names. A large and fearsome tabby became General Tom Forster. Tom was an inveterate poacher brought home somewhat battered after his forays by a kindly gamekeeper, Ned Dodd, who often covered up my sins and those of my lawless animals. A teddy bear was hastily re-named Perry Widdrington, but later became Edward, the reason escapes my memory, perhaps the Widdringtons had gone out of favour. Dolls had not the appeal for me that teddy bears and animals had: Perry, alias Edward, is still with me, somewhat moth-eaten and decayed by the ravages of time.

For a child brought up on a farm I was curiously innocent and firmly believed that I had been found in a cluster of Michaelmas daisies. This perhaps is not so astonishing as it sounds when one realises that the great discovery of the nineteen-sixties was sex; no explanation had been given how procreation was achieved before the age of discovery. I asked my father, in mixed company, of course, being a tactful child, how he knew the difference between boy and girl lambs. He told me, by their wool; I accepted this astonishing information without question. Daddy told me, so it must be true. I was rather puzzled when Blueboy, having been regarded as a male for five years, produced a littler of kittens in the boot-cupboard. One of this surprising family was given the ghastly name of Adolphus. He died young.

I was born on a Michaelmas Day before the First World War at Lipwood Well near Haydon Bridge in the South Tyne Valley and there appears to be confusion in some people's minds on this very ordinary and I should have thought uninteresting subject.

There are four houses in the district prefixed by Lipwood which adds to the confusion. Lipwood House (now Hall), High Lipwood and Middle Lipwood. My uncle William Ridley came to Lipwood Well in 1897 and when my father married, William returned to his father's farm at Peel Well. The latter is now in ruins. Until 1926 my father farmed four of these farms as well as the 'out-by' land at Seldom Seen (appropriately named) and The Dam Fell. Lipwood Well is a mile and a half west of Haydon Bridge, close to the A69 which runs parallel with the Newcastle-Carlisle railway line, now threatened with closure.

My birth-place was recorded in the Pipe Roll of the sixteenth century; the name of the tenant then was Mason. The farms mentioned were at one time Derwentwater property, confiscated after the '15 Rebellion by the government and administered by the Greenwich Hospital Commissioners. That my beloved third Earl of Derwentwater once owned my house roused my abiding interest in this most tragic of Northumbrian Jacobites. I had no idea then what a Jacobite was but I determined to become one and still am in my sympathies for those who 'came out' in the '15 and the '45.

Though born on Michaelmas Day I was so small and delicate that it was January before I was christened in the beautiful little church of St Cuthbert at Beltingham. It is reputed that Nicholas Ridley, the Marian Martyr and the most famous Ridley of all, received his baptismal name at Beltingham. This is possibly so, as in the sixteenth century the Ridleys were the most powerful clan in South Tynedale and Beltingham was their domestic chapel.

My father was over forty when he and my mother married, so I feel I am a generation behind, as he was able to tell me so much about his childhood and the stories which had been handed down by his father. It is difficult at times to be certain that I

3

experienced events or if they were told to me. My father was a wonderful story teller and a superb mimic, a talent, if that is the right word, which I have inherited but, like my father, I cannot mimic people I love. I cannot, as he could, make myself look like the person he was mimicking. He would have loved Mike Yarwood!

The first stories I remember were about a family of rabbits who lived in a burrow close to the South Tyne. I could go to the exact place now, though the swing bridge where I so often played has gone. According to my father, Mr Rabbit always took the children for a walk along the riverside on a Sunday morning while Mrs Rabbit was cooking the dinner. She was renowned for her delicious Yorkshire puddings. So convincing were the Rabbit sagas that I believed every word! No wonder my favourite books were those of Beatrix Potter. I cannot remember learning to read, not even 'the cat sat on the mat'. My mother read aloud to me every day; *The Coral Island* was one of my favourites, closely followed by the perennial *Black Beauty* — even now I dissolve into floods of tears when I think of 'Ginger'. *Children of the New Forest* naturally appealed to my historical interest, as did a rather sentimental effusion called *Little Arthur's History of England*. In case the reader assumes I was a child prodigy, which I never was, I mispronounced every other word much to the embarrassment of my parents.

My mother was a completely different character. Intensely practical, it was she who curbed my flights of imagination and encouraged the literal down-to-earth attitude which I possess to a high degree. In later life it was sheer joy to go on expeditions with her. She loved to see beautiful homes and treasures and was never envious. Any outing with her was an adventure. If I have criticism of my early upbringing it was that I was over-protected so that when hard times came I found it extremely difficult to adapt to changed circumstances. In those days criticism of one's parents was one of the unforgivable sins, the result was that parents were not like other people. It was not until the Second World War that I discovered that my mother was a woman in her own right! One of the good things that has come out of the social upheaval people of my generation have witnessed is that children and parents have a much more balanced relationship.

When I look back objectively, if it is possible to do so about oneself, I have a feeling of warmth and security which has been sadly lacking in later life. To be truthful, there was a serpent in my Eden, a serpent in the form of a boy cousin who had a disruptive influence on the entire household. Why did I dislike, even hate, this child so much? Was it because my father disliked him? These are questions which can never be answered. Before I was born my mother gave birth to a boy who died in infancy. This tragedy, as it must have been to my parents, was never mentioned, which makes me wonder if my mother lavished affection on her nephew as a compensation for the loss of her son and did my father resent this? Someone asked me the other day if my father ever called me by a boy's name and I had to admit he did. I was always Thomas to him, never Nancy, and he once told me that had I been a boy he would have wished me to have been a land-agent.

Certainly this unwanted cousin's vists brought conflict with him, conflict which at the time I was unable to understand. Like many children then and now I wished he would die. Incredible though it may seem he did! My only emotion was profound relief that he wouldn't be coming to stay any more. How cruel can children be! I played happily with the other children, some of whom became life-long friends, though I was sent home in disgrace from a children's party when I had attacked a horror who looked like Little Lord Fauntleroy. He had golden curls and I took great joy in pulling them almost to their roots. This exploit did not meet with parental approval. Savage instincts must have been curbed as I was later described as having the best manners of those who atttended the children's dancing class which was held in Haydon Bridge Town Hall.

I have said enough about the little girl who was mounted on a green cushion and fell under the spell of Prince Charlie. I have no intention in succeeding chapters of describing either private or public life in detail. I am not referring to diaries or a catalogue of events and I am astonished when I read some autobiographies how the writer can recall the most trivial happenings in such chronological order. I have a very good memory, but there are many gaps in my recollections. This book is not an autobiography: it is about history and how I came to experience it and have a life-long affair with it although I am not an historian. I learned about history from places and people and the chapters which follow are not in the ordinary chronological order which is found in school books. They come in the order in which history happened to me.

My father was the inspiration of it all, though I am sure that in no way did he try to mould a small girl's ideas. He was passing on to me the interests and ambitions which had lain dormant throughout his own life. As I was only eighteen when he died, I was unaware that my abiding love of history, tradition and patriotism (now a dirty word) were his legacies to me. The idea that these legacies would ever be put to practical use never occurred to me. More than thirty years were to pass until I fulfilled what must have been a smouldering desire to put into spoken and written words all that my ever loving and understanding parent had inspired.

CHAPTER TWO

CHILDHOOD AND BEYOND

Heather land and bent land,
And valleys rich with corn,
God bring me to Northumberland,
The land where I was born.

Wilfrid Gibson

THE FIRST CHAPTER to this book may have given the reader an impression that as a child my only interest was history and that I was a precocious little prig who had no other interests. Prig I may have been, that is for others to decide, yet I had many other interests and my life was full and varied. My mother did her utmost to avoid my becoming a spoilt child. Sometimes, looking back, I think she went to the other extreme and was more strict than she would have been had I been one of a family of brothers and sisters. My father, too, chastised me severely if I tried to be a little show-off. I can remember being sent to my room when I announced at a luncheon party that Northumberland was the most beautiful place in the world. With the crushing remark, 'You have never been anywhere else,' I was ordered from the dining-room and spent the rest of the day crying in the nursery, my only companion a blue Persian cat.

I was a tearful child and taking me to Newcastle must have been a nightmare. In those days the newspaper boys were bare-footed which upset me greatly, and the sight of a lost dog brought fresh floods of tears. My exasperated mother was driven to distraction by these outbursts of grief and once told me (I remember it was in Grey Street, close to the Monument) that the dog responsible for this emotional outburst had more sense in its tail than I had in my whole make-up! I remember a money box which had a little drawer which pulled out when the

7

pennies overflowed. This was my Doctor Barnardo's collecting box, and I also sent money to a Mission in Stepney. This may have been because I had a 'courtesy aunt' who was Matron of a London hospital. My mother did a great deal of work for the Red Cross and I had a doll named Isabel which my mother dressed as a Red Cross nurse. This must have been about the time when I first heard of Florence Nightingale, little dreaming that in the years to be I would give a talk about The Lady with the Lamp.

Not only was I a tearful child, I was also mischievous and some of my escapades were not smiled upon by the adult world by which I was surrounded. Every day before lunch my father had a glass of whisky and soda and on one occasion he nodded off to sleep. I had been playing with my paint-box and creeping up behind my unsuspecting parent I painted his bald head green! Again I was sent upstairs. I was an inveterate climber (now I can't bear heights) and once barricaded myself in the grocery cupboard. I refused to be 'talked down' and threw a packet of rice at the onlookers. Unfortunately for me it hit my father. This was too much for an upstairs punishment and to my great humiliation I was put into the yard so that when the men came back to the stables after their midday dinner they could witness the downfall of 'the little varmint', as Watson our head stockman called me. In spite of being called a 'varmint' I loved Watson. On the terrible night when my father was dying I ran to Watson's cottage in the darkness to seek help. Watson came back with me, bringing Moss, the dog, and the man and dog who spent their lives in the service of the Ridleys were in the bedroom when the end came.

I loved my home and the land passionately and like all children thought that nothing would ever change. How wrong I was! The truly rural way of life is declining before one's eyes. In the name of progress farming is no longer a way of life; many of the farming fraternity of today have no love for the land, to them it is a factory and animals are machines. The innovations which horrify me most are these deplorable experimental 'farms' where foetus transplants are carried out. Nature will hit back, but unfortunately it is the poor beasts who will suffer for

8

the greed and worship of Mammon which characterises these perpetrators of unnatural operations. Many farmers are now business tycoons under the cloak of agriculturists. Due to their machinations wild life and the genuine countryside are fast disappearing. Hedgerows are flattened, trees felled, historic farm buildings such as gin-gans are demolished. For the uninitiated a gin-gan is a circular building supported by stone pillars where the threshing of the corn which separated the grain from the chaff was done. The primitive 'machinery' was propelled by a horse walking in circles, reminiscent of a treadmill. Surely preservation orders should be imposed to prevent vandal-minded farmers from such acts of destruction. Conservation and wildlife societies have been formed in an endeavour to preserve what is left of the country of my childhood.

Three memories of my childhood years stand out vividly. There were the summer evenings when the corncrakes lived up to their name; one could always be heard in the East Haugh at Lipwood Well. It is years since I heard the unmistakable 'croak' and years since I have seen a kingfisher. I remember the winter evenings when I lay tucked up in bed with Little Ted, a very battered teddy bear whose photograph is in my bedroom today, and listened to the owls in the Lees wood. An old body in Haydon Bridge told me the owls hooted because their feet were cold and I believed her. Best of all was hearing the men come to fother (fodder) the horses in the stables and loose boxes. The hurricane lamps the men carried shone like great cat's eyes in the darkness. Blueboy, the Persian cat, lay in front of the dying fire; coal fires were lit in the bedrooms in the winter. Now it is another cat, Alec, who sleeps in my room and lies beside an electric fire.

Many of the memories I have revived may appear to be trivial but to a child those days were all important and as I grew older and went further than Northumberland I found my homing instinct had strong roots. Home to me means the Lipwood Well of long ago: the years spent in Newcastle upon Tyne now appear unreal and Wylam I regard as a base, I do not belong there and never will. I cannot bear to pass my old home, it is neglected and squalid and has an uncared-for and unloved look. Some of my friends have the sensitivity to by-pass the house for me, others do not. The beech hedge has gone and the 'orange blossoms' my mother planted have withered and died. The cart sheds have been demolished and the garden is a shambles. I have a photograph of my home as it used to be and it is almost impossible to believe it is the house that was loved and cared for and knew so much happiness all those long years ago.

The Round Plantation has survived and I am reminded of it every time foot and mouth disease is mentioned. When I was very young there must have been an outbreak of this most vicious infection somewhere in Northumberland and my quick ears picked up remarks about 'Stand Still' orders and the uses of disinfectant. I had no knowledge of what it really meant but in some way I gathered that animals had to be killed. Not knowing that it attacked only cloven-hoofed beasts, I laid my plans to evacuate my entire menagerie to the Round Plantation. How I was to transport and hide the vast number of refugees presented no problems to me in spite of numbers, food and, above all, secrecy. My score was two dogs, twenty-one cats, two horses, a canary, some bantams and, of course, myself. Mercifully for all concerned the plans were never put into operation; the alarm must have died down. I think I rather liked the idea of leading an army and as it was about the time I discovered Shakespeare (through *Lamb's Tales*) I no doubt longed to cry, 'God for Harry, England and Saint George'!

With the entry of Shakespeare into my life was born another abiding love — poetry. I loved Scott's *Marmion*, did and still can reel off the now despised Kipling. Those who denigrate patriotism should read *If* and try to carry out some of the principles the poem so forcibly recommends:

> *If you can walk with crowds and keep your virtue,*
> *Or walk with kings nor lose the common touch;*
> *If neither foes nor loving friends can hurt you,*
> *If all men count with you but none too much;*
> *If you can fill the unforgiving minute*
> *With sixty seconds' worth of distance run,*

Yours is the earth and everything that's in it,
And which is more, you'll be a man, my son.

Surely here is an example for those today who seem to have no standards to guide them.

In adolescence I devoured Rupert Brooke and having strong Jacobite sympathies I revelled in the ballads of William Aytoun. As I stood at the door of the vault where Bonnie Dundee is buried at Blair Atholl, the lines came into my head:

Strike! and when the fight is over,
If ye look in vain for me,
Where the dead are lying thickest,
Search for him that was Dundee!

The bullet-proof jacket Dundee wore at Killiecrankie which, alas, did not save his life is preserved at Glamis Castle in Angus.

Some people, and there were many of them, criticised my up-bringing. 'Filling the child's head with nonsense' was one denunciation. The nonsense was in later life to become my career and my means of living. The know-alls were to be proved wrong. I must now make a confession. I was never educated in the full sense of the word. I never went to school! I was taught at home by an excellent governess who now lives in Darlington. Pattie, as I affectionately called her, used to take me to the Roman Wall. Sometimes we walked, sometimes I rode my pony; my mother was a wonderful picnic organiser. A favourite part of the Wall, where I have spent many happy days, was the stretch from Steel Rigg Gap to the summit of the Whinshields Crag, the highest point over which the Wall travels. I have stood on the summit and looked west to where, when visibility is good, the Solway can be seen. The name fascinated me. I have always loved names and I planned that one day I would explore the Scottish side of the Firth and go to Dundrennan where the unhappy Queen of Scots spent the last night in her kingdom. Like many of my dreams that has come true.

For the child who never went to school, if one excepts a kind of Dame Trot establishment for young 'ladies' which I endured for two years, it is a miracle that I have been able to support myself. My only academic qualification is in speech training. I chose this subject as from an early age I had an intense interest in poetry and drama and developed the ability to imitate local accents. This so-called ability was very much frowned upon by my parents and neither would have appreciated my talk on dialects of Northumberland. As I grew older much of my interest in dialect faded: I now understand my parents' point of view. In fact I have developed an aversion to dialect and have no desire to be remembered for my Northumbrianisms. It is with my love and knowledge of history that I wish my name to be associated.

Dancing lessons I adored, first in the Town Hall at Haydon Bridge, then in Corbridge, where we paraded round the room to 'The Teddy Bears' Picnic'. French lessons were not such a success, though I did manage to make a Paris taxi driver understand that I could read *meters!* To finish me, in more ways than one, I was sent to London to be shown the sights, taken to theatres and generally polished up by my courtesy Aunt Alice. I still have the letters my parents wrote to me. My father was then an invalid and I think missed me greatly but he was determined that his 'Thomas' should have every advantage within his power to give. I travelled to King's Cross in the 'Queen of Scots' Pullman and the young of today will be amazed to hear that I was put in charge of the guard and told not to speak to strangers. One of our maids warned me against the White Slave Traffic, which I thought had something to do with Uncle Tom's Cabin. Mine was a curiously innocent generation. When I returned safely from the Big City I was for the first time a guest at what was then described as a society wedding. The reception was at Langley Castle, the home of the bride's aunt. Many years later I stayed with the bride in Berkshire and she gave me much valuable information on the restoration of Langley about which I devoted a chapter in *A Northumbrian Remembers* (Robert Hale, 1970).

My memory is curiously selective: I have an amazingly good memory for whatever may be my greatest interests and an appallingly bad one when it comes to mundane affairs. So far age has not dimmed my memories, the happy ones I treasure, the unhappy are in my subconscious and both can be roused by the smallest incidents. A song of the war years, 'I'll Walk Beside You', recalls what might have been, while tunes from Gilbert and Sullivan's *H.M.S. Pinafore* evoke memories of my father shaving in the mornings in the bathroom at Lipwood Well. He always sang when he shaved. The smell of lilies-of-the-valley take me home again to where those enchanting flowers grew close to the beech hedge. When I dreamed my dreams in that garden half a century ago I little thought that all the history I had been told, the expeditions we had made and the political knowledge I gained were one day to become my way of life. I must long ago have broken Queen Elizabeth the First's record of sleeping in strange beds. 'Nancy Ridley slept here' could cover most of Scotland, every English county but four, Jersey, The Isle of Man, France, Italy, Holland, Belgium, The Republic of Ireland, Denmark, Canada and the United States of America where I found a link with Flora Mcdonald. The country girl has gone a long way.

In 1930 my whole life changed. My beloved father died, worn out by ill-health, the effects of the slump (now called a recession) broke him; that and his never-ending generosity to many who did not deserve it. It is still too painful to write about the goodbye to my home — I was never to know complete security again. It was then that my indomitable mother decided that we should make a new life in the city of Newcastle upon Tyne and we lived there until her death in 1950. My great regret is that I had not started my career as a speaker and writer in her lifetime. I had no inkling that I could do either. Where my gifts, if one may call them so, came from I will never know. Genes go back a very long way and the creative instinct may have come down through the generations from some long forgotten ancestor. When I was a child there was an old lady living in Haydon Bridge, whose name was Hannah Wray, who claimed to have 'the Sight'. She prophesied that one day I would be famous. That has not come true, but I have kept the Ridley flag flying often in the face of almost unsurmountable disasters. I admit I am ambitious: that trait I have inherited from my grandfather Matthew Ridley of Peel Well. All that I am is the result of my upbringing and the examples set by both my parents. To them I owe everything that is good in me. Some may well ask where the bad side comes from: for that I can blame only myself.

History was not forgotten when I lived in Newcastle. I bought an Austin Seven for £57 and my mother and I travelled the country, always with an object in view. The first journey in BVK 972 was to the Carter Bar, the scene of the Raid of the Redeswire in 1575; then, growing very daring, London was the next target. We spent hours in Westminster Abbey and the Green Park. These pre-war years were happy and fruitful. I had gained my diplomas in Speech Training and had taught a future High Court Judge to read and write. I am not attempting to describe the war years, they have been over-written. All I will say is that I was on duty on the W.V.S. Canteen on number nine platform when the troops came back from Dunkirk. It was a memorable day, and one would have thought we had enjoyed a glorious victory rather than a mass evacuation judging by the behaviour of the troops. They were hanging out of the windows, waving and singing, dressed, or partly dressed, in some curious assortments of uniform. They were not Scottish troops but 'Loch Lomond' was their theme song. They kissed every girl in sight and one soldier shouted, 'We're the only lot left in the league.' The British are indeed a strange race. It was the voice of Winston Churchill that gave us the courage that helped us to endure. One could sadly ask where is that spirit now. I drove a huge Bedford truck which masqueraded as an ambulance. Mercifully for the injured I never had a passenger. Driving in an uncontrollable truck up Westgate Hill in the black-out was not for the nervous or injured.

In 1940 I joined the Postal Censorship and was there until the war in Europe ended. Looking back now I realise that the amount of report writing I did was an excellent training for the embryo writer, boring though it was at the time. The city and county were invaded by His Majesty's Forces and many a long-suffering 'foreigner' was press-ganged by me to travel by bus or on foot to my beloved Beltingham, to Blanchland and Dilston and, like it or not, was compelled to listen to the

14

Derwentwater story. Allen Banks and Plankey Mill were the sites of many a press-ganged picnic. One Royal Air Force officer asked if this Earl of Derwentwater I talked about so much was a friend of mine!

I have been amused, and also deeply hurt, by the 'unauthorised biographies' I have heard and endured over the years. It would seem that I was born old and am a queer old woman who writes unreadable books, gives talks to Women's Institutes only (I am on Christina Foyle's list of Speakers) and never had any fun. (I have had so many boyfriends that I cannot remember who they all were.) The happiest year of my life was 1945, the year in which I was 'the only girl in the world'. This is one of the closed chapters of my life which I have no intention of reopening.

When my mother died in 1950 another chapter in my life closed. From then on I have lived with and for history. The people who most interest me and whose lives I have studied are the subjects of the ensuing chapters: they are my friends, their haunts are mine, and the journey is not over yet.

CHAPTER THREE

DERWENTWATER: A VERY GALLANT GENTLEMAN

With me the Radcliffe's name must end,
And seek the silent tomb;
And many a kinsman, many a friend,
With me must meet their doom.
And when the head that wears the crown,
Shall be laid low like mine,
Some honest hearts may then lament
For Radcliffe's fallen line.

Derwentwater's Farewell, Surtees.

IT IS INEVITABLE that I should write and speak about my most dearly loved Northumbrian, James Radcliffe, third Earl of Derwentwater. Born in a house which was once his property and hearing stories of the '15 from my father and my governess I have been familiar with the Derwentwater story since earliest childhood. A four-poster bed in the west bedroom at Lipwood Well was reputed to have come from Dilston Castle where James Radcliffe lived. When my life at Lipwood Well left me the bed sadly had to be sold. I sometimes wonder where that bed is now and if the owner is aware of its history. Lord Derwentwater and Dorothy Forster from Bamburgh, the heroine of the '15, became my friends. One doll of mine was dressed by my mother in what I imagined Dorothy would have worn. Accuracy didn't worry me in those days and I no doubt saw some pictures in a fancy dress magazine, very popular when I was a child, and chose a costume I admired, probably in the wrong century.

When I was dragooned, not persuaded, to do some public speaking more than twenty-five years ago, I had no difficulty in deciding what my first talk was to be about. It had to be the

16

Derwentwater story. I have often been asked why I chose to be a speaker, and my reply is that I didn't choose, this part of my life was decided for me. An old boy friend coerced me, telling me that as I was mad about history and had two diplomas in speech training, it was obvious where my talents lay. For some time I refused to listen to the idea of appearing before an audience: the very thought filled me with horror. Then came the ultimatum, a booking was arranged without consulting me and I gave my first talk to what will ever be a nameless Women's Institute! I was in such a state of nerves that I told the story of my favourite Northumbrians in a manner which would have given them cause for surprise had they been able to hear me. Though I have travelled a long road since then I am always nervous and always feel I could have done better. It must be a wonderful feeling to be pleased with oneself, an experience I have never achieved.

Dilston on the Devil's Water: Blanchland, that most historic and enchanting village on the Northumberland-Durham border: and Bamburgh — all associated with the Rebellion — were some of the first places I visited and have continued to visit throughout the years. I have written and spoken at length about Derwentwater's romance with Dorothy Forster, which I am omitting in this chapter, concentrating on Lord Derwentwater and the part he played and the price he paid for his part in the ill-starred Rising to restore a Stuart to the throne of Great Britain.

Dorothy Forster's epic ride to London with the Warenford blacksmith, whom she eventually married, makes her one of Northumberland's most heroic women and I feel the reality of her daring effort has been lost in the world of romance: she has not received the place in history she so richly deserves. Tom Forster's escape from Newgate was made possible by the courage and resourcefulness of his sister. Brother and sister lie side by side in the crypt of Bamburgh Church.

Whenever I pass Dilston today, and throughout my life I have done so on countless occasions, I think of the young man who rode out so long ago to die far away from the lands he had come to love so dearly. He has become a legendary figure in Northumbrian history. Books, some fact, some fiction, songs and ballads have been written about 'The Bonnie Earl'. His memory is still green today and Dilston will for ever be associated with this young man who lost his life for his loyalty to the House of Stuart. In the short time he spent in Tynedale James Radcliffe must have made an impact on the district out of all proportion to his ties with the county; in fact one could almost describe him as an 'incomer' and Northumbrians, even today, are wary of 'foreigners'.

By Northumbrian standards the Radcliffes would be regarded as a new family. It was by marriage that the family acquired vast estates in Northumberland and Cumberland and it was not until 1616 that Sir Francis Radcliffe built the castle above the Devil's Water at Dilston. Only a ruined tower and the chapel are left standing and for many years the tower has been in a sad state of decay and neglect.

James Radcliffe was born in London in 1689 and his short life ended on Tower Hill on a cold February morning in 1716. He was the eldest son of the second Earl and his wife Lady Mary Tudor. Lady Derwentwater was an illegitimate daughter of that great and illustrious founder of many of the aristocracy, Charles II. Why Tudor was chosen to be the surname of 'Lady' Mary is unknown, it seems an incongruous name for a Stuart to adopt. Lady Mary's mother, Moll Davis, was an actress and no doubt the Monarch's roving eye discovered her at some playhouse. It was through this relationship on the wrong side of the blanket that the fate of James Radcliffe was sealed. His cousin was James, the Old Chevalier, and claimant to the throne of Britain, therefore blood and destiny confirmed his allegiance to the ill-fated House of Stuart and 'The King Over the Water'.

James Radcliffe was educated in France with his cousin and as the marriage of his parents was not a happy one he spent little or no time in England until after the death of his father, when he succeeded to the earldom and came home to Dilston. It was in 1710 that all Tynedale and most of the Northumbrian gentry gathered at Dilston to welcome the Bonnie Earl. As is still the case today, most of the well-known Northumbrian familes were related and Swinburnes, Widdringtons, Claverings, Erringtons

18

and many others were there to meet him.

As one travels through Northumberland legends and mementos of the '15 are found in unexpected places. Near Slaley is a holly bush which Jacobite agents are said to have used as a hiding place for messages. The Swinburne ladies of Capheaton are said to have disguised themselves as fairies and hidden letters under four stones, hence the name of Fourstones village today. I wish I had the fertile imagination so many writers possess. A cave under Shaftoe Crags was a hiding place for Derwentwater when he was a wanted man: he is also said to have taken refuge in the priests' hiding hole in the Lord Crewe Inn at Blanchland, where Tom and Dorothy Forster were living at the time. The Forsters' Aunt Dorothy had married Lord Crewe, Bishop of Durham, and what is now one of the most attractive inns in Northumberland was then used as a hunting lodge by the Bishops of Durham. Callaly Castle in the north of the county was then in the possession of the Claverings and in the drawing room (the house is open to the public) are two blank spaces on either side of the fire place. The intention was that when the Stuarts were successful in regaining the crown medallions of the Old and Young Chevalier would be placed there. Not far from Callaly is Eslington, from where George Collingwood rode out for the last time when he joined the Jacobites.

When Derwentwater rode out to join the Rising he reined in his horse near Beaufront where a farm named Mount Pleasant stands and from where there is a most glorious view of Dilston and the Water of Tyne and the moors that roll south towards Blanchland. The horse was not the 'bonnie grey steed' of Surtee's ballad —

And fare thee well, my bonnie grey steed,
That carried me aye so free;
I wish I had been asleep in my bed
Last time I mounted thee.

The bonnie grey steed had been sent to a Mr Hunter for safety, the Government having decreed that horses owned by Roman Catholics above a certain value were to be confiscated. The

19

letter Lord Derwentwater wrote to Mr Hunter concerning the horse is now at Nunwick, near Simonburn. The 'steed' was a mare, and there is a picture of her in existence. The ghost of Anna, the Countess who threw down her fan challenging her Lord to give her his sword, is said to have been seen by many people, as she haunts the banks of the Devil's Water. A bridge over the burn is known as the Earl's: it was the last resting place for his coffin which was brought from London, travelling by night. Hunstanworth near Blanchland claims to have been the last resting place in Durham.

Mercifully none of us can foresee the future. The rejoicings at Dilston and Hexham for the Earl's return were kept up for days and all seemed set fair for the future. James Radcliffe could never have dreamed that he would become a legend. His time was spent in getting to know his tenants, visiting and receiving visits from friends and neighbours: in other words living the life of a great landlord and country gentleman but with a difference. He did not speak the Northumbrian tongue as everyone of whatever class did in those days, neither did he drink himself under the table, as 'gentlemen' were all three-bottle men. He was of medium height, slightly built and remarkable for his gentleness and good manners, which were not an outstanding feature of the Northumbrians of the eighteenth century! He set about building a great house at Dilston where he could bring his bride. He married Anna Webb from Dorset and spent two years away from Dilston as part of an arrangement demanded by his father-in-law.

When he returned to his beloved Tynedale with his wife, the storm clouds were gathering and time was running short. His Countess appears a rather shadowy figure, little is written about her apart from the fact that she belonged to an old Roman Catholic family, was an ardent Jacobite and became the mother of two children. Surely she must have loved her new home and there is no doubt she was devoted to her husband.

A frequent guest at Dilston was the Earl's brother Charles. He, too, many years later met the same fate as his brother. After the Rebellion of the '45 he became the last Englishman to be beheaded by the axe. Charles was an extrovert, wild and impulsive, and even when a prisoner in Newgate after the '15 kept up his high spirits and managed to escape from the hell of Newgate and reach the continent. James and Charles became familiar figures in Northumberland, playing bowls at Stamfordham was one of their pastimes and the house and garden where they played are still there.

It was on the first of August 1714 that the storm broke. Queen Anne was dead and immediately the Whig Government brought from Germany the Elector of Hanover, who was crowned George the First — a thoroughly unpleasant character who couldn't speak a word of English. The Scots dubbed him 'the wee, wee German Lairdie'. The Act of Settlement of 1701 had decreed that only a Protestant could sit on the throne of Britain and James Stuart, Queen Anne's half-brother, was a Catholic. From then on until the defeat of the Jacobite armies at Preston, the supporters of the House of Stuart were on the run. Many and varied were their hiding places: they were proscribed men. When the Scots raised the Standard on the Braes of Mar, the scene was set for the '15. On a golden October day the Bonnie Earl came 'out'. The fatal mistake of making Tom Forster the general of the untrained raggle-taggle army was made. The reason this decision was taken was that it would attract more recruits if the army were led by a Protestant squire, even though incompetent, rather than a Roman Catholic Earl. Tom Forster was not endowed with brains though he was one of the two Members of Parliament Northumberland sent to London. Lack of brains could apply to many Members today. No qualifications are required by candidates, which is very obvious in some cases. Lunacy, I understand, is one of the few barriers to standing for election, but I have serious doubts if that bar is always exercised! Tom had no military experience, was headstrong and self-opinionated, which was emphasised by his surrender at Preston to Generals Willis and Carpenter before consulting older and wiser men.

On the wild hills of Wanny where the Wansbeck rises the Northumbrians mustered; from there they marched to Rothbury and proclaimed King James the Third. From the capital of Coquetdale General Forster marched his pathetic little army to Warkworth where he and Lord Derwentwater stayed in The Mason's Arms, a pub which still exists, and their brief stay is recorded on a beam. From Warkworth to Morpeth was the next stage in their progress. Bad news greeted the Rebels, as the Government termed them. Newcastle had shut its gates; big business meant more to the merchants of Newcastle than a forlorn cause.

A great deal of valuable time was wasted in marching to and fro between the market towns, then General Forster turned north possibly encouraged by the fact that forty Scots under a brother of the Earl of Home had joined the Northumbrians at Warkworth. Crossing the Border, forces were joined at Kelso, one of the loveliest of the Border towns. On the 22nd October, with drums beating and pipes playing, the combined armies took the road for Longtown and into England, pausing at Brampton. The gallant but already doomed men made a short stay in Alston where Derwentwater had property. Through Kendal and on towards Shap they struggled, rather than marched. The long, weary climb to the summit of Shap in November must have been heartbreaking for men and horses.

When at long last they neared Preston in Lancashire there was a struggle, as always, to persuade the Scots to cross the Ribble. Nothing made any difference now, the '15 was over before a shot was fired. Well-trained, well-fed Government troops surrounded the town and, although the Jacobites were prepared to fight to the death, they were compelled to surrender. Every man but one was taken prisoner, and he was Frank Stokoe from Chesterwood, near Haydon Bridge. Retribution was quick and merciless. Many of the rank and file were hanged without trial in the Lancashire prisons. The nobility and gentry, as they were termed, were taken to London, the Lords to the Tower, the commoners to Newgate.

I am fortunate to have in my possession a beautifully bound little book published in 1868 by T. Allan, Newcastle upon Tyne, entitled *The History of the Earl of Derwentwater and the Rebellion of 1715. A Full Account of the Earl's Early Life; His Rising in Rebellion; Surrender at Preston; Trial; Speeches; and Execution. With Many Interesting Details of Other Northern*

Gentlemen Who Took Part in The Rebellion. The price of this most informative 'life' was sixpence, by post sevenpence. This treasure was given to me by the late Sir William Gibson, together with *The Heirs of Dilston and Derwentwater*, by S. S. Jones, printed in 1869 and, to quote, 'Hexham. Printed at The Courant Office, Market Place.' In this case no price is mentioned. The following Articles of Impeachment of High Treason are taken from one of the precious books.

PROCEEDING
IN WESTMINSTER HALL
UPON THE
IMPEACHMENT
AGAINST

James Earl of Derwentwater, William Lord Widdrington, William Earl of Nithisdale, Robert Earl of Carnwath, William Viscount Kenmure and William Lord Nairn.

Die Jovis 9 Februarii, 1716.

About One a Clock the Lords came from their own House into the Court erected in Westminster Hall, to pass Sentence upon James Earl of Derwentwater, William Lord Widdrington, William Earl of Nithisdale, Robert Earl of Carnwath, William Viscount Kenmure and William Lord Nairn, in the manner following.

The Lord High Steward's Gentlemen Attendants, two and two.

The Clerks Assistant to the House of Lords, and the Clerk of the Parliament, with the Clerk of the Crown in the Court of Chancery bearing the King's Commission to the Lord High Steward.

The Masters in Chancery, two and two.

Then the Judges.

The Peers Eldest Sons, and Peers Minors, two and two.

Four Serjeants at Arms with their Maces, two and two.

The Yeoman Ushers of the House.

Then the Peers, two and two, beginning with the youngest Barons.

Then four Serjeants at Arms with their Maces.

The Serjeant at Arms attending the Great Seal and Purse Bearer.

23

*The Garter King at Arms; and the Gentleman Usher of the Black
Rod, carrying the White Staff before the Lord High Steward.
The Lord High Steward alone, his Train born.*

> *When the Lords were placed in their proper seats, and the Lord
> High Steward on the Wooll-Pack,*
> *The Clerk of the Crown to the Court of Chancery, standing
> before the Clerk's Table with his Face towards the State,
> having His Majesty's Commission to the Lord High Steward
> in his Hand; made three Reverences towards the Lord High
> Steward, and on his Knee presented the Commission to the
> Lord High Steward; after which the usual Reverences, the
> same was carried down to the Table; and then Proclamation
> for Silence was made in this manner:*

*O Yes, O Yes, O Yes! Our Sovereign Lord the King strictly charges
and commands all manner of Persons to keep silent, upon pain of
imprisonment.*

> *Then the Lord High Steward stood up and spoke to the Peers.*

*Lord High Steward. His Majesty's Commission is going to be read;
Your Lordships are desired to attend.*

*All the Peers uncovered themselves, and they and all others stood up
uncovered while the Commission was reading.*

GEORGIUS R.

James Radcliffe knew his fate was death but his courage and
integrity never faltered during the farce the King and
Government called a trial. Attempts were made to soften the
King's heart — all to no avail. Lady Derwentwater, who was
pregnant, went down on her knees, begging German George to
spare her husband's life. 'No mercy' was the King's doctrine, a
policy carried on by Butcher Cumberland at Culloden in the
'45.

The Bonnie Earl died as he had lived, bravely and with
dignity. He wore a black velvet suit which is still preserved, and
he was seen to shake only slightly as he prepared to die. On the
24th February 1716 James Radcliffe passed into history. That
night the Northern Lights were so bright in the Corbridge
district that for many years they were known as Lord
Derwentwater's Lights.

*Fearful lights, that never beckon, save when kings or
heroes die.*

In the last century a granite cross was erected to the memory
of James and Charles by Mr C. J. Bates of Langley Castle. It
stands on the roadside between Haydon Bridge and Langley
and bears the inscription:

> *To the memory of James and Charles*
> *Earls of Derwentwater*
> *Viscounts Langley*
> *who were beheaded on Tower Hill*
> *for loyalty to their lawful sovereign.*
> *24th February 1716 and 8th December 1746*

This is their only memorial in Northumberland.

CHAPTER FOUR

THE FLODDEN STORY

We'll hear nae mair lilting at our ewe-milking;
Women and bairns are heartless and wae;
Sighing and moaning on ilka green loaning —
The Flowers of the Forest are a' wede away

Jane Elliot

ALL MY LIFE names have held a fascination for me and when at an early age I discovered Sir Walter Scott's *Marmion* I was enthralled by the Battle of Flodden Field and memorised the 'roll of names' and deafened anyone who had time to listen to me with my self-styled 'accomplishment':

Then thundered forth a roll of names:
The first was thine, unhappy James!
Then all thy nobles came;
Crawford, Glencairn, Montrose, Argyll,
Ross, Bothwell, Forbes, Lennox, Lyle —
Why should I tell their separate style?
Of Lowland, Border, Isle,
Fore-doomed to Flodden's carnage pile,
Was cited there by name.

My first opportunity to visit Flodden Field came after a day spent at The Royal Highland Show at Kelso. In those days the Highland, like its counterpart the Royal in England, went on tour each year. Now both shows have permanent sites; the Highland at Ingliston near Edinburgh and the Royal at Stoneleigh in Warwickshire. Economics forced the Societies into their abandonment of the 'Grand Tour' which I think was a retrograde step and my interest in both events has waned.

The thrill of crossing the Border with my father to that Highland of long ago which was to lead me to Flodden is still with me. The excitement and the anticipation of such an expedition into a 'foreign' land built up for weeks and I was too excited to sleep on the night before the great day dawned. For reasons which I cannot recall my mother did not go with us, perhaps she had too much of *Marmion* and her daughter's histrionics. An uncle, long since dead, was with us and the driver of a hired car, a Cubitt which I believed was akin to a Rolls Royce! We left Lipwood Well at crack of dawn with strict instructions to come home early for my nine o'clock bedtime. These admonitions fell on deaf ears and our reception when we did return was frigid in the extreme.

I cannot believe that all this happened more than half a century ago: I can remember the exact details of my new dress. The dress was made by Miss Boyd in Haydon Bridge and was of pale yellow cotton with a slotted belt of broad brown ribbon. My hat was a white panama with elastic which cut my chin, white socks and brown sandals completed my outfit. I thought I was very grand with my Brownie box camera and a small suede handbag which another uncle brought from Dublin for me and which I called my 'Dublin puss'.

The Show was held beside the Tweed, a river I dearly love. Kelso and Tweedside hold many happy memories for me. Naturally most of the time at the Show was spent with the Border Leicester sheep of which my Grandfather once had a pedigree flock. It was on that long ago day that I heard about the Highland Clearances. My father, who had been talking to a breeder from Sutherland, told me that it was the Northumbrians who were responsible for taking the sheep to the Highlands and not, as so many historians affirm, the much abused Duke of Sutherland. The Robsons of North Tyne imported the indigenous Northumbrian Cheviots (sheep, not hills) and to distinguish the English from the Scottish the latter are termed North Country Cheviots to this day.

We must have left Kelso fairly early as Flodden was the real purpose of the outing, the Highland was merely a curtain-raiser. I cannot remember exactly where we crossed the Tweed into England; I think it must have been near Carham, a name which was to mean much to me in later years, not at

27

Coldstream which I now know so well. As it was June the days were long and the sun was still strong when at last we came to the wicket gate which guards the steep path to Piper's Hill. At such an early age I was unable to understand that Flodden was a tragedy. That it was the saddest battle ever fought on Northumbrian soil I was to realise in the years that were to be. That fatal field became as poignant to me as Culloden is in Scotland. The essential difference between the two battles is that though both sides fought to the death there were no calculated atrocities carried out after Flodden. The unpleasant Earl of Surrey was humane in comparison with 'Butcher' Cumberland after Culloden. The Borderers indulged in what was their way of life, 'lifting' (a euphemism for looting) and burning as they made for home. What did impress the child of long ago and was written on her heart for all time is the inscription on the granite cross.

To the Brave of Both Nations. 1513.

Flodden was the first battlefield I had ever seen. Little did I dream that one day I would talk and write about King Jamie and the men who died with him, or that a friendship would be formed which resulted in my becoming a writer. My great regret is that neither my father nor my friend of later years, Hubert Blenkinsopp Coulson, lived to share in whatever success I have had. Like the Flowers of the Forest 'they are a' wede awa'.

No such thoughts were in our minds when my Father decided that it would be a good idea to come home by Gretna Green! Gretna was miles out of our way and necessitated our crossing the Border again and following the road to Hawick and Mosspaul in the heart of Border country. Disregarding our instructions to arrive home early we went to Gretna Green. I still possess a hideous china ornament representing the Smithy where runaway marriages took place. I thought the horror was beautiful and as horrors often do it has survived the passage of time while exquisite ornaments have been broken.

When we left Gretna my father was ready for a meal and a drink. I was too excited and tired even to think about food. A terrible disappointment was in store for Daddy and my uncle: the only pub (I'm sure the more dignified name of hotel would be used then) still open was temperance! Both my father and grandfather had an aversion to temperance hotels, an aversion which I share. My father loved his whisky, a taste which his daughter has inherited, preferably a good malt! A somewhat deflated party returned to Lipwood Well and the welcome was restrained. Too tired to care I was sent to bed with my teddy bears and animals to dream of Flodden and, with the inconsequence of a child, of Cheviot sheep that marched to war!

Many years later I met the man who used his considerable influence to encourage me to write. I have written about H.A.B.C., as I called him, in *Northumberland Then and Now* (published by Robert Hale, 1978). This man, who was responsible in literally forcing me to become a writer, was born at Carham-on-Tweed where his father was Vicar. Later the family moved to Branxton which is where many of those who fell at Flodden are buried, and before the battle ended took their last stand in the churchyard.

I will now attempt to describe what I have learnt throughout the years of the actual battle; its cause, its glory and undying memory. Only last week I passed the road-end to Branxton and had a distant view of the cross on Piper's Hill. I have memorised the Flodden prayer, which is as follows:

> *O Lord Jesus Christ, who didst stretch forth thine arms*
> *upon the Cross to draw all men to Thyself, we beseech*
> *Thee that, as Thou hast given peace to the peoples of*
> *our own land, so Thou wilt give peace to all nations,*
> *and to the homes and hearts of all who dwell on earth,*
> *for Thy Holy Name's sake. Amen.*

Flodden was fought on 'Black Friday', the ninth of September, 1513, when all the flower of Scotland died; a date written in blood on the pages of Border history. The great Sir Walter immortalised the battle fought on that misty September afternoon in his epic 'Marmion' which, as I have said, was my introduction to Flodden. His descriptive pictures in verse are probably as accurate as any ever written. There were no historians such as Froissart to leave first-hand descriptions for posterity, and a certain amount of conjecture is inevitable. I am no military historian and had I been it is impossible to estimate the strength of the opposing armies: what is indisputable is that the losses on the Scottish side far outnumbered those of the English. In 1913, four hundred years after Flodden, the Episcopalian Church of St Mary and All Souls was built in Coldstream on the Scottish side of the Tweed, the 'Souls' commemorating the nameless men who so gallantly died for Scotland and King James. A touching and worthy tribute.

In 1513 the English King, Henry VIII, was waging one of his many forays into France and the Scottish King, James IV, seized the opportunity to march against the 'auld enemy' and ravage the Borders. It is ironical that Louis XII's Queen was the sister-in-law of the Scottish King. There is a story, that could possibly have substance, that the French Queen sent James a glove challenging him to attack her native England. Mary Tudor, as she had been, was a pawn in the political marriage market and heartily disliked her aged and dissolute husband. All her life she had been in love with Charles Brandon, Duke of Suffolk, whom she married after her first husband's death and in due course became the grandmother of the ill-fated Lady Jane Grey. These intricate relationships bear a likeness to a charade. The Queen of Scots was born Margaret Tudor and therefore both Queens were sisters of English Henry! After the ghastly slaughter of James on Flodden Field, his widow married 'Archibald Bell-the-Cat', as the Earl of Angus was known. It was this Earl of Angus with whom James quarrelled before the battle began and 'Bell-the-Cat' escaped the holocaust. The Queen of Scots and her new husband took refuge in Harbottle Castle in Coquetdale and there was born a baby girl who grew up to marry the Earl of Lennox and become the mother of Darnley. Deep concentration is necessary to disentangle these intricate relationships!

The Scottish Army marched from Scotland's capital with drums beating and pipes playing in late August after the harvest was gathered, little realising they were marching to their doom and their requiem would be the haunting 'Flowers of the

Forest'. The Scotsmen crossed the Tweed into England a little way upstream from Coldstream and James was entertained in Ford Castle by the young and attractive Lady Heron, her Lord having crossed into Scotland to brawl with his enemies the Kers. Sir Robert Ker met with a nasty 'accident' at the hands of Lord Heron.

James IV, in keeping with his Stuart blood, had a roving eye and critics say that he loitered too long at Ford. Others affirm that Lady Heron was a spy and used all her charms on the susceptible King, thereby allowing the English intelligence, which was very efficient, to summon all resources as speedily as possible. The Earl of Surrey was at Pontefract and immediately made for the north, joined by the Bishop of Durham and his private army. He was then reinforced by the famous Stanley Archers who landed at Tynemouth. The Northumbrians, always spoiling for a fight, strengthened the English army which encamped on Barmoor Bridge and, to quote Sir Walter:

> *Even so it was, from Flodden Ridge*
> *The Scots beheld the English host*
> *Leave Barmoor Wood, their evening post,*
> *And heedfully watched them as they crossed*
> *The Till by Twizel Bridge.*

The bridge over which Surrey took his artillery is still in use today but plans are afoot to build a new bridge some distance from the original to carry today's heavy traffic. Surrey was so old and infirm that he was carried in a litter.

James IV drew up the Scots on Branxton Hill facing Scotland whilst Surrey ultimately drew up the English between the Scots and Scotland. Most of the two armies fought hand-to-hand and the Scots, who appear to have lost all control, kicked off their brogues and dashed down Branxton Hill, only to be mown down by the Stanley Archers. When the Scottish dead were buried most of them were bare-footed. Flodden was history within hours, the King fought bravely and, like all his race, knew how to die. His hands had been severed, yet he stood his ground with his nobles round him until they were all slaughtered.

31

Till utter darkness closed her wing,
O'er their thin host and dying King.

The King's body was taken by the English to Berwick where it was placed in a lead coffin and rests far away from Scotland in Sheen Abbey, though there are conflicting opinions as to his final resting place.

In 1952 a Festival Committee was formed in Coldstream by a voluntary committee, not by the Town Council, to hold a Civic Week in August and at the same time commemorate Flodden. Premature though the ceremony is, the pilgrimage to the battlefield is impressive and poignant. The week begins with the Sashing of The Coldstreamer by the Provost. The Coldstreamer is elected by secret ballot and chooses his Right-Hand Man and his Left-Hand Man, who hold their offices for a year. The procession, led by The Coldstreamer, leads a field often a hundred strong of The Coldstream Riders' Association into England and along the narrow road to the wicket gate, the entrance of the steep path to the Flodden Memorial on Piper's Hill. The granite cross was erected on a piece of land given by John Carnaby Collingwood Esq. in 1910.

The Coldstreamer and his two men doff their bonnets and accompanied by a piper place a wreath at the base of the cross. Inevitably the lament is 'The Flowers of the Forest'. The ceremony over, the cavalcade then climbs the hill to Flodden Edge where a short service is held and an oration read by a local V.I.P. When I was present at the ceremony the oration was read by the Earl of Haddington.

At the Edinburgh Tattoo of 1978 the Casting of the Colour, which is part of the Selkirk Annual Common Riding, was most beautifully enacted and it appealed to me more than the other episodes of that memorable Tattoo. The 'Casting' dates from Flodden when out of eighty Selkirk men who fought with the King only one returned. His name was Fletcher and he was one of five brothers. When he came home after the battle he cast down a blood-stained English banner and this ceremony has continued through the ages. At the Tattoo the massed bands played 'Blue Bonnets over the Border'. The Casting of the

Colour captured the imagination of BBC's Nationwide programme and was televised in February 1981, the first of a new series showing Festivals of Britain. Surely 'festivals' is a misnomer in this case — Selkirk is commemorating a tragedy.

My sympathy with the Scots is obvious; the English army was largely composed of the southern English and although Northumbrians have fought with the Scots in the past we are more akin to the Lowlanders than to people south of the Trent.

As long as history is written the memory of Flodden will never be forgotten. The second verse of 'The Flowers of the Forest' epitomises the tragedy.

Dool and wae for the order sent our lads to the Border!
The English, for ance, by guile wan the day;
The Flowers of the Forest, that fought aye the foremost,
The prime of our land, lie cauld in the clay.

CHAPTER FIVE

GRACE DARLING, NORTHUMBRIAN HEROINE

Eternal Father, strong to save,
Whose arm hath bound the restless wave,
Who mad'st the mighty ocean deep
Its own appointed limits keep,
O hear us when we cry to Thee
For those in peril on the sea.

WHEN I WAS a child there hung in the dining-room of my grandfather's home at Peel Well a horrifying picture of a shipwreck. This dramatic scene fascinated me and I remember asking endless questions about the identity of the lady and gentleman, as I politely described them, who were looking so tidy and calm in the midst of gigantic waves with a storm-tossed ship in the background. One of my aunts told me that the lady's name was Grace Darling and that she and her father had been very brave and rowed their boat from a lighthouse called the Longstone to rescue survivors from a sinking ship named the Forfarshire. Many years were to pass before I sailed to the Longstone in very different conditions from those experienced by Grace Darling. Through the years Bamburgh, where Grace was born, has been familiar ground for me and I have attempted to unravel the myths and legends which have accumulated round this famous Northumbrian girl of long ago and to describe as accurately as possible the event which made Grace Darling a national heroine. On one of the few summer days of nineteen eighty-one I made yet another pilgrimage to Bamburgh with the object of writing this chapter and so absorbed was I in the past that a long-suffering friend had to rescue me from the middle of the road where I was standing, oblivious to the cars milling round me. The past, not the present, had become reality.

In 1815, the year of Waterloo, there was born to William and Thomasin Darling their seventh child, who was christened Grace Horsley. Her birthday was 24th November. The birthplace of the heroine still stands, bearing a plaque to commemorate the event. At the time of her birth Grace's father, William Darling, was an assistant lighthouse-keeper on the desolate Brownsman Island. When the birth was imminent Thomasin Darling came to the mainland to the house of her father Job Horsley who was employed as a gardener by the Crewe Trustees. The Horsleys were of good Northumbrian stock, while the Darling family had its origins on the Scottish side of the Border. It was in the ancient church of St Aidan that the baby girl was christened. St Aidan's is one of the most beautiful and historic churches in Northumberland, a county once described as 'the cradle of Christianity'. In December 1815 the Darlings were re-united as a family on the Brownsman where they stayed until 1826 when William Darling became the keeper of the new light, the Longstone on the outermost island of the archipelago of the Outer and Inner Farnes. These scattered islands are an outcrop of the Great Whin-Sill which is the provincial name for basaltic rock.

Thus from infancy the sea was Grace's constant companion and boats were the only form of transport she knew, divided as she was from the mainland by the North Sea or German Ocean as it would be known then. The mainland was to her a view of 'the lordly strand of Northumberland, and the goodly towers thereby'. The 'lordly strand' is as glorious a sight today as it was to the lighthouse-keeper's child of long ago. The great fortress of Bamburgh still stands firmly upon its mighty rock, impressive as an Arthurian legendary castle. Life was isolated and austere. Basic foodstuffs such as flour and bacon were provided by Trinity House, augmented by the few vegetables that could be grown in the sparse soil and the fish and fowl abundant in and around the islands. William Darling also grazed a few sheep which would be slaughtered in 'the backend', as autumn is termed in Northumberland, and salted down for the winter. The family was a self-sufficient entity which must have had a great deal of influence in forming Grace Darling's self-reliant and resourceful character which was revealed in her heroism in the hour of disaster.

There is no concrete evidence that Grace received any formal education though there is some indication that she attended a school in Spittal near Berwick for a short time. Her handwriting and command of English are evident in surviving letters which are on display in the museum in Bamburgh which bears her name. She was a good needlewoman, cook and housekeeper — there was no time for idleness in the lighthouse home. When the children were old enough they took their turns in keeping watch, attending to the lamp and manning the cobles, those fishing boats peculiar to the Northumbrian coast. The coble in which Grace and her father made their historic voyage, now named Grace Darling, has been preserved and is one of the most interesting exhibits in the Museum.

As the family was composed of four girls and three boys Grace would never be lonely, and one can visualise the closely knit group gathered round the fire, father reading aloud to them, for William Darling was a self-educated man with a fund of knowledge, unusual for a man in what the nineteenth century would regard as his lowly station in life. Mrs Darling, too, was highly intelligent. Twelve years older than her husband she made him a devoted wife and was a loving and caring mother. The dominating character in the family seems to have been the eldest sister named Thomasin after her mother. She was seven years older than Grace and, if her portraits are good likenesses, she must have been a formidable woman. It is extremely difficult to know which of the many portraits of Grace really resemble her — certainly not the horror which was my first introduction to her! Judging from her clothes in the Bamburgh Museum she was tall and slim, her bonnets and dresses are charming as is her finely tucked christening robe. It is amazing that so many personal items have been preserved. Although life on the Brownsman was isolated there were many trips to the mainland to visit relatives, calls would be made upon the family by Trinity House officials and passing boats would anchor to exchange news with the family.

In 1826 the move to the Longstone was made, and the light on the Brownsman discontinued. The new lighthouse was modern, with more living space and it was promotion for William Darling to be appointed keeper. Electrically operated now, the Longstone is still a guide and warning to shipping, situated as it is close to jagged, cruel and dreaded Harcar rocks which have claimed so many lives. To study the situation of the Longstone and its surroundings an ordnance survey map or Admiralty chart is essential but to realise fully the dangers of this off-shore island one must go oneself to appreciate the hazards of this most dangerous sea-way. I have stood on the Longstone when the sun was shining and the sea calm as a millpond, so I can only imagine what it must be like to be there when a gale-force wind is blowing.

Grace was eleven years of age when she came to her new home and for the next twelve years her life was uneventful. She grew up to be a quiet, modest young woman, leading a somewhat circumscribed life. The family dispersed, leaving only her brother William Brooks as a contemporary and she appears to have resigned herself to an island life. By the standards of those days the Darlings were affluent. Trinity House paid William the elder £70 a year plus a gratuity of £10. The Crewe Trustees rewarded him financially for the reporting of wrecks, life-saving and salvage work. Their living expenses were few and above all they were content with their lot.

In 1838 came the dramatic wreck of the Forfarshire which was to change Grace Darling's whole life and make her a heroine of history. The Forfarshire is described as a packet-steamer of 150 tons burden and 200 horse power, plying between Hull and Dundee and the Captain, James Moncrieff, 'is appointed to sail as under weather, etc. permitting'. She was registered at Dundee. It was a Captain Humble who was in command when the ship left Hull on the 5th of September, 1838. There were no weather forecasts then and the only signs of trouble came from the ship's boilers, which were leaking. It seems incredible that this state of affairs was not discovered or rectified before leaving port; these points were raised at the subsequent enquiry. It has never been confirmed how many passengers the ship carried in addition to cargo and crew — every account differs. What is factual is that on the night of 7th September, when the ship was off the Berwickshire coast, the engines failed and the vessel started to drift south. The Captain made sail but misjudged, it is surmised, his course, which he had set for the Inner Farnes. The seas were tremendous and gale-force winds were blowing when in the early hours of Thursday morning the Forfarshire struck the Big Harcars and broke her back. The Captain and his wife, who was travelling with him, went down with his ship.

At a quarter to five that morning Grace, who was looking at the storm from her bedroom window, saw the wreck. Mrs Darling had just finished her watch, as William, the younger, was spending the night at Seahouses. In spite of using strong binoculars (if that is the correct nautical expression) it was not until about seven o'clock that it was light enough for the watchers to see figures clinging to the rocks. Like the unfortunate Captain Humble, William Darling misjudged events. He assumed that neither the Bamburgh nor the North Sunderland lifeboat would put to sea in such a tempest, and he made the decision that with the help of his twenty-two year old daughter he would make an attempt to reach the survivors. Helped by Mrs Darling and Grace the boat was launched and this middle-aged man and young woman set out on their immortal voyage. I have not enough nautical knowledge to describe their route in detail, only to state that due to the heavy seas they rowed for more than a mile to cover the short distance of 300 yards which separates the Longstone from the Harcar rocks. Contrary to the many exaggerations expressed in words and on canvas Grace used only one oar! No woman could have used two oars of the weight and size of the original which can be seen in the coble 'Grace Darling'. She must have been given superhuman strength to achieve what she did: her courage requires no embellishments. When the reef was reached nine people were found alive. Grace held the coble steady while her father managed to bring five people aboard. Then began the terrible return trip to the Longstone, but make it they did, and William Darling and two of the survivors struggled back to

38

bring the remaining four still marooned on the Harcars, while Mrs Darling and her daughter did all they could to warm and feed the rescued.

More people were to crowd into the lighthouse that September day. The North Sunderland men had put to sea after hearing a warning gun fired from the lookout at Bamburgh Castle. Unable to launch the lifeboat the North Sunderland men, with William Brooks Darling among them, manned a fishing vessel, taking more than two hours to reach the wreck. They were too late to save any lives and brought three bodies off with them. It is no criticism of Grace Darling's courage, nor in any way denigrating her claim to glory, yet I cannot help feeling that the North Sunderland men deserved more praise and recognition than they have received and this is an opportunity to record their names to be added to those many indomitable Northumbrians who have gone down to the sea in ships. The lifeboat cox who took command of the fishing vessel was William Robson, with his two brothers James and Michael, Thomas Cuthbertson, Robert Knox, William Swan and Grace's brother Brooks as crew. That there was strong feeling at the time was apparent and the North Sunderland people remained withdrawn and censorious of the general acclamation.

The aftermath of the disaster had repercussions, not all of them happy. Rumour and speculation were rife, and the press published conflicting accounts. The results were to involve many people: the first inquest was so unsatisfactory that a second one had to be held. An enquiry apportioned blame often on false premises: Lloyds, Trinity House, The Hull and Dundee Shipping Company, insurance companies and private individuals heard and gave evidence. The summing-up was inconclusive. For a full and detailed account I can strongly recommend *Grace Darling and Her Times* by Constance Smedley, published in 1932. Several books have been written on the subject but many **are** so confused and biased and exaggerated that one must decide which is the best and ignore the others. *Grace Darling* by her sister Thomasin and D. Atkinson is factual, though exceedingly difficult of access.

After the rescue Grace Darling had only four more years to live. I cannot help wondering if the publicity and adulation which made her a national heroine, comparable only with that given to a 'pop' star today, were too great for a humble, unassuming young woman who had hitherto led an almost cloistered existence. The strain must have been intolerable to one who valued privacy. The Longstone became a Mecca. Artists, some good, some bad, flocked to the island to paint her portrait: poets, mostly indifferent, churned out some of the most ghastly verse it has ever been my lot to read. Her correspondence was voluminous, her name was toasted in London, at banquets, boats were named after her, offers of marriage poured in and, true to tradition, demands were made for locks of her hair, china souvenirs were proudly displayed on 'what-nots' — Grace was in danger of being commercialised. That she did not lose her head is a miracle; she remained the same uncomplicated, simple Northumbrian girl and was slightly contemptuous of the sensationalism. Not one souvenir was ever in the Darling household and none are in the possession of her descendants.

At the instigation of the third Duke of Northumberland, The Royal Humane Society granted Grace a gold medal, but not before the Cities of Edinburgh and Glasgow each gave her one of silver. A fund was promoted and subscriptions were numerous. The Darlings had no experience of such affairs and very sensibly the Duke (to a Northumbrian there is only one Duke, it is quite unnecessary to add the patrimony!) had appointed himself the guardian of the heroine's affairs and, being a just and fair man, saw that the North Sunderland men received some monetary recognition. Before His Grace took charge of the Darling affairs Grace made one great mistake, which was that of accepting an invitation to exhibit herself at a circus in Edinburgh! The promoter of this extraordinary plan was the owner of the circus, who was later accused by the ladies of Edinburgh of diverting money given by them ostensibly to a fund for Grace into his own pocket. Mercifully Grace discovered the deception in time and did not suffer personal humiliation.

40

Early in 1842 Grace's health was causing her family anxiety and she came ashore to stay with her sister Thomasin in Bamburgh. She was never to live on the islands again. Duchess Florentia, the wife of the third Duke, now took even more interest in her husband's ward and established Grace as her protegée. It is typical of the class distinction of those days that when Grace and her father were summoned to Alnwick to be received by their Graces and presented with a watch, the father and daughter were taken to the servants' quarters for refreshment. Medicine, too, had its rules as rigid as those of class. Any ailment that could not be diagnosed would be cured, it was believed, by a change of air. Grace was sent to Wooler, 34 miles from Bamburgh, and prescribed quantities of goat's milk. Not surprisingly, the patient showed no signs of improvement and was then installed with Thomasin in a small house in Prudhoe Street in Alnwick (Prudhoe is one of the Duke's many titles). Town life had no appeal for Grace and soon she and Thomasin came back to the house in Bamburgh where so soon she was to die. It was an uncanny feeling to be in that house not long ago: it is now a shop where I bought picture postcards.

On the evening of 20th October 1842 Grace died in the arms of her father. She was twenty-six. Her untimely death was attributed to tuberculosis but my firm conviction is that her public killed her. She is buried beside brother Job in Bamburgh churchyard. Yet she was not allowed to rest in peace. Subscriptions were raised to erect a memorial to her memory on the Inner Farne, contributions coming from the young Queen Victoria and her mother, the Duchess of Kent. The Bamburgh people demanded that the memorial must be in Bamburgh and they had their way. A Victorian monstrosity was erected, a horror which crumbled away only two years after its erection. Nothing daunted, more money was raised for its restoration and much of the stone was brought from Cragside. In 1893 this inappropriate memorial was demolished by a gale. Unfortunately, another 'resurrection' took place and today there is an effigy of Grace with the famous oar by her side, recumbent on a massive stone plinth with an elaborate canopy above her. Far more appropriate and poignant is the plain stone monument in the restored chapel of St Cuthbert on the Inner Farne which bears the simple inscription:

To the memory
of
Grace Horsley Darling
a native of Bamburgh
and an inhabitant of these islands
who died Oct. 20 A.D. 1842
Aged 26 years.

CHAPTER SIX

DUCHESS SARAH

And Anne shall wear the crown but Sarah reign . . .
Churchill shall rise on every Stuart's fall.
And Blenheim's tower shall triumph o'er Whitehall.

A Tory lampoon

WHEN I MADE the discovery that Sarah Churchill's favourite servant's name was Ridley, a personal interest in the life of The Terrible Duchess became an exhaustive study. Countless biographies of Sarah have been written but in spite of endless research little is known of her faithful companion and confidante Grace Ridley. When David Green's book *Sarah, Duchess of Marlborough* was published in 1967 (by Collins), I wrote to him for information and he told me that he, too, had been unable to discover more than the fact that Grace was the daughter of a clergyman. Many Ridleys have entered the Church but few have left their native county. I have not yet given up hope that one day I may uncover the mystery of this much esteemed servant.

In her will The Terrible Duchess left to Grace a fortune of £16,000, a striking watch, a miniature of Marlborough and a picture of herself by Kneller. When David Green's book was written this picture hung in the gallery at Earl Spencer's Northamptonshire family seat at Althorp. Sarah's second daughter Anne married Charles Spencer, Second Duke of Sunderland, so it is probable that Grace Ridley on her death left the picture to her late mistress's daughter. The Spencer-Churchill connection was to prove historic. In 1807 the names were incorporated by law, the most famous to bear the hyphenated name was, of course, Sir Winston. The Princess of Wales, Lady Diana Spencer, is a descendant of the woman who nominally ruled England for many years. How proud the ambitious Sarah would have been, had she known her line was to achieve royal status.

Sarah had in common with Sir Winston a strong sense of the dramatic. The country's greatest war leader declared that he had arranged to be born on St Andrew's Day. This he announced in a broadcast commemorating Scotland's patron Saint Andrew and I recall the programme vividly. Broadcasting with the then Prime Minister was Sir Harry Lauder, who broke into his famous song, 'Keep right on to the end of the Road'! It was obvious that the two old warriors had been toasting St Andrew in his national drink! Sarah 'arranged' to be born in the year of the Glorious Restoration, one week before the King came into his own again. Through six reigns, from the days of the Divine Right of Kings (Queen Anne was the last sovereign to carry out the ritual of touching for the Queen's evil) to the days of the great commoners, foremost of whom was Walpole, Sarah lived for most of her long life in a blaze of publicity and dramatic situations.

Born Sarah Jennings, her parents were small gentry, one of the many Royalist familes impoverished by the Civil Wars. By a coincidence land owned by the Jennings family was in the manor of Churchill in Somerset. Very little is known of Sarah's early life. It is not even certain where she was born; that it was in Hertfordshire, probably near St Albans, is proved by a Cathedral Register, discovered in 1880, which gives the date of her christening as June 17th, 1660. There are records to show that the Jennings family lived at Holywell House near St Albans during Sarah's childhood and it is reasonable to assume that is where she was born. In later life she spent a great deal of time at Holywell, near the village of Sandwich, and displayed affection for that part of Hertfordshire until the end of her life.

I cannot help feeling sympathetic towards Mrs Jennings, left a widow at an early age with a family of seven (some say five) children to provide for. Today the future Duchess would have been deemed a problem child. She soon showed signs of the arrogant and ambitious side of her character which was to intensify with age. She had the hot temper associated with red-haired people, a temper which eventually was to be the cause of her fall from grace at Court. There is no doubt that she was an intelligent child with a quick and active brain, yet she was virtually unteachable. Although spelling had not yet been standardised Sarah's was unique, as her letters reveal. At a time when ladies of quality were expected to speak fluent French Sarah could, and would, speak only her own language. For one who has heard Sir Winston's interpretation of foreign languages in his broadcasts, it is impossible to refrain from speculating on the influence of heredity. French and German were mutilated by Sir Winston Spencer Churchill. I cannot help wondering if an eighteenth century Duchess and a twentieth century Prime Minister were so intensely proud of their British ancestry that they had a veiled contempt for foreigners which they expressed by refusing to learn any language other than their own.

Until the emancipation of women, the only way for them to exert any influence was to be the power behind a man. In those class-ridden days the best way to achieve this end was to secure a place at Court, and by some means Mrs Jennings had managed to obtain a position for her elder daughter Frances in the household of the Duchess of York. Frances Jennings was a beauty; Sarah's looks are better described as striking, in keeping with her character. How thankful Mrs Jennings must have been when in 1675 Sarah followed Frances to London. The curtain had risen for the girl from Hertfordshire and for many years her life was to be lived in the limelight of the world of politics, intrigue and the struggle for power. She was an extrovert and an exhibitionist with a personality that defied all opposition.

As a result of her appearance at Court she became the companion of two little girls who were both to become reigning queens. Mary and Anne Stuart were the daughters of James, Duke of York, and his first wife, Anne Hyde. The stepmother of the future queens, Mary Beatrice of Modena, was younger than they were! Before her official appointment Sarah had met briefly both the Princesses, now she was to become the favourite of the younger, Princess Anne, who was eight years her junior, and they formed one of the most famous freindships in history until Sarah's banishment from Court. Perhaps to some these two entirely different young women are better remembered as 'Mrs Morley' and 'Mrs Freeman', names which they themselves devised, Sarah choosing to be Mrs Freeman as she said her nature was more open and frank than that of her royal mistress. Sarah never suffered from an inferiority complex! The Restoration Court was not conspicuous for its moral standards and it is to the credit of Princess Anne and Sarah Jennings that they were to be acknowledged as of virtuous character. Some contemporary writers go as far as to affirm they were the only two!

In the household of the Duke of York was a page named John Churchill and there he met and had an affair with the notorious Barbara Castlemaine. This appears to have been the only clandestine affair in which John Churchill ever indulged. As Barbara was sharing her favours with the King at the same time, it was unfortunate for the future Duke of Marlborough that he was caught *in flagrante delicto* by the King in the Castlemaine's bedroom. Churchill is reputed to have jumped out of the window, the King throwing his trousers after him. This undignified exit had a surprising sequel. Barbara paid off her young lover to the tune of £5,000. With the wages of sin he bought an annuity and founded his fortune. Writing of his ancestor, Sir Winston in his inimitable manner simply says, 'John Churchill was a prudent young man'.

The Churchills were an old Royalist family and had arranged a suitable marriage for their soldier son, but 'Mrs Freeman' had already attracted the attention of Barbara's cast-off lover. It was marriage or nothing for Sarah and in 1678 they were secretly married in the presence of the Duke and Duchess of York. It was a marriage which was to last for forty-six years. In spite of Sarah's storms and tantrums she loved her husband passionately, a love which John reciprocated. When on duty and often abroad he wrote to her every day, letters which she kept all her life. After the death of the great Duke, Sarah wrote in her memoirs that she had read and re-read all his letters but could not bring herself to burn them. Sarah was frank in the extreme and recorded in writing that 'my lord pleasured me with his boots on'.

46

Five children were born in rapid succession, four girls and a boy, who died of the dreaded smallpox when he was only sixteen. He had been destined to follow his father's military career. The death of Lord Blandford was the greatest tragedy in what could be described as their private lives. Smallpox, too, claimed the life of Elizabeth Churchill who married the Earl of Bridgewater. The dukedom which Queen Anne bestowed on John Churchill was inherited by his daughter Henrietta, who had married the son of Godolphin; thus the descent is through the female line.

After the death of Charles II, the troubled reign of James II was to have a serious effect on the Churchills. Created an English Baron by the new King, Churchill accompanied his royal master to Scotland by sea, a voyage which nearly cost them their lives when their ship, *The Gloucester*, was wrecked. Later on another Scottish visit Sarah joined her husband in Edinburgh, John travelling to the Border town of Berwick upon Tweed to meet her. In the three years of James's reign Churchill was playing a double game, one which I have never been able to reconcile with his previous record of loyalty. Outwardly supporting the Catholic King, he was involved in plots with the Protestant Dutch to depose the unpopular monarch. That the Princess Anne was involved in these intrigues to bring over Dutch William and her sister Mary there is no doubt. Bigot though James was, he was her father and I find it impossible to condone the part Anne played in bringing about his downfall.

When William eventually landed in England and the forces of James were defeated, it has to be admitted that the future Queen and her friends the Churchills were determined to be on the winning side and Churchill deserted the unhappy James. Anne, one has to remember, was dominated by Sarah at the time; the stronger character overcame any scruples the weaker woman possessed. I detest Dutch William, and am not ashamed to say that I take an unholy delight in telling the story of Sir John Fenwick's horse, Sorrel. Sir John Fenwick of Wallington in Northumberland was loyal to James and was tried and executed as a traitor and his horse Sorrel was confiscated by the

47

King. One day at Hampton Court the Dutchman was riding Sorrel when the horse caught a hoof in a mole hill and stumbled, unseating his rider, who was not in good health at the time and, in no state to suffer shock and injury, he died shortly afterwards. After William's death Jacobites drank a toast to the little gentleman in the black velvet jacket!

With the accession of Anne in 1701 the Churchills became the most powerful family in the country. Sarah became not only the power behind the man but also the power behind the throne. Many ambitious schemes and intrigues were planned with John's advancement in view. It was no exaggeration to dub the future Duchess as Viceroy Sarah. The Queen made her Mistress of the Robes, Groom of the Stole and Keeper of the Privy Purse. When the War of the Spanish Succession erupted John was made Captain General of the Forces. Whatever one may think of some aspects of his character John Churchill was one of the most outstanding military commanders of all time. The might of England became legendary. The very names evoke a sense of patriotism: Ramillies, Malplaquet and the glorious victory of Blenheim, fought on the Danube far away from England, are enshrined on the battle honours of the British Army.

During these long absences of her beloved John and without his guiding influence and caution Sarah became more and more autocratic and domineering. A dedicated Whig and Low Churchwoman, she endeavoured to impose her views on the Tory and High Church Queen. One of Sarah's many failings was that she would never forgive or forget, or admit that she had been wrong. Quarrels and reconciliations with the Queen were becoming endemic and were faithfully recorded in her memoirs. Storm clouds were gathering, but not before by the Queen's generosity the Churchill daughters had been well endowed and Sarah was contemplating the building of a London house on the land which the Queen had given her. That dream house was eventually built by Wren and named Marlborough House. Centuries later it was the home of Queen Mary in her widowhood.

When the Wars ended the Queen created John Churchill

Captain General, first Duke of Marlborough and gave him the much coveted Garter. Parliament and a grateful nation made their magnificent contribution of money and land on which to build the Palace of Blenheim. The following is an extract from the Chief Guide's office at Blenheim written in answer to one of my queries '... Blenheim Palace is built on Crown Lands (presented by Queen Anne). The Marlboroughs retain this on condition that each year, on the anniversary of the Battle of Blenheim, each Duke of Marlborough shall take or send to the reigning sovereign or his or her personal representative at Windsor Castle a replica of the personal standard of Louis XIV. This is now known as the Blenheim Standard...' The library presided over by David Green, who wrote the excellent official guide, is the most gracious room in this astonishing palace.

The vicissitudes endured by the designers and builders of the Marlboroughs' Palace would fill a tome. I am not surprised that Vanburgh had a nervous breakdown. Sarah demanded estimates for the smallest details; like John she was 'prudent' concerning money affairs. In her lists of expenditure, along with trifling amounts, there is an entry that 4,755 yards of curtain material was ordered at a cost of £2139. In her old age she dictated an inventory of Blenheim from memory including such items as sixty-seven dozen table napkins and ninety-three table cloths of the best sort!

I found Blenheim overwhelming and flamboyant, with an atmosphere reminiscent of 'Viceroy' Sarah. The famous tapestries depicting Marlborough's victories are magnificent and greatly impressed me. I felt a thrill of pride when the guide mentioned the great landscape gardener Capability Brown as the man responsible for the construction of the lake and part of the parkland. 'Capability', or Lancelot as he was christened, was a Northumbrian boy of humble parentage born at Kirkharle. He received his rudimentary education at the village school in Cambo.

All human beings are complex and contradictory and the meticulously minded Sarah could be extremely kind and generous. She founded Alms Houses at St Albans, and the wretched small boys who were used as chimney-sweep 'brushes' were rewarded with new suits of clothes and a golden guinea. Ironically, it was this kind side of her nature which brought about her downfall. A poor relation named Abigail Hill, later to be Mrs Masham, was brought to Court by Sarah and by means of the backstairs gained the friendship and patronage of the Queen. When the final break came and Sarah was deprived of the key to the Privy Purse, it was Abigail who usurped Sarah and became Keeper of the Privy Purse. There is no more dangerous enemy than one who has been a bosom friend and, not content with the humiliation of Sarah, a plot was hatched by John's enemies, Bolingbroke and Harley, portraying John as a traitor and for some time the hero of Blenheim was a prisoner in the Tower. It was, in today's language, a frame-up and for lack of concrete evidence Churchill was released and he and Sarah went into what she described as 'voluntary exile' on the continent. With perfect timing they returned on August 2nd, 1714, the day after the Queen's death.

The next few years were spent in supervising the building of Blenheim, which was delayed by lack of money. John was dead before its completion. The days of glory were over and in 1722 Sarah's Great Duke died at the age of 72. He was buried in Westminster Abbey with the pomp and circumstance his contribution to his country's power so richly deserved. After Sarah's death his body was brought from Westminster to Blenheim to lie beside his Duchess in the tomb which she designed. Its overpowering figures and ornate design did not appeal to my taste.

In the twenty-two years as a widow Sarah earned and deserved the name of The Terrible Duchess. Quarrels with her children occupied a great deal of her time. Only one daughter, Mary, Duchess of Montague, outlived her mother. Litigation was a favourite pastime of The Terrible Duchess and she must have been her lawyer's chief source of income. Her will was changed so many times, as new beneficiaries and so many codicils were added, that this must have been a perpetual occupation. Her correspondence and her memoirs were a prodigious achievement and added to this voluminous literary task was a record of 'The Misdemeanours of my Grandchildren'. Once when looking through a desk she found strands of her red-gold hair which she had cut off in one of her quarrels with John, knowing that he loved her beautiful mass of hair and that this demonstration of displeasure would hurt him deeply. He had treasured this until his death. Yet this is the same woman who, when the Duke of Somerset, the 'Proud' Duke, proposed to her after John's death, told him, 'If I were young and handsome as I was, and not as old and faded as I am, and you could lay the whole empire of the world at my feet, you would never share the heart and hand that once belonged to John Churchill'. She was indeed a most extraordinary mixture, capable of intense love and intense malice.

As she grew older and her health deteriorated, her spirit remained the same. Grace Ridley must have been a saint to suffer the startling changes of mood. When Sarah heard a doctor discussing her illness with Grace she exclaimed, 'I won't be bled and I won't die.' The world had left her: long ago 'Viceroy' Sarah had become a memory. She lavished affection on her many pet dogs and the few friends left. In the year before the '45, on 18th October 1744 at the age of 84 Sarah left the scene in which she had played such a dramatic role. The only announcement was in the London Gazette in the brief words, 'The Duchess of Marlborough died last night'. Her tumultuous 'reign' had ended.

CHAPTER SEVEN

CHARLES II, PORTRAIT OF A MAN (Part I)

The twenty-ninth of May
Is Royal Oak Day.
If you don't give us a holiday,
We'll all run away.

WHEN THE CHILDREN of long ago chanted this rhyme few, if any, realised they were commemorating the birthday of the most brilliant monarch who has sat on the throne of this country. Certainly when I was a child I had no idea of the significance of the date until it was explained to me by my father and later by my governess. Charles II was born in the Palace of St James on the twenty-ninth of May 1630 — a year after the dissolution of Parliament. Thirty years later in the year of the Glorious Restoration he returned to his capital city of London on his birthday after nine years of exile: the King had come into his own again.

I cannot remember with certainty when my intense interest in this Stuart monarch was born; that it was many years ago, more years than I care to remember, is the only certainty and my interest in the character of this outstanding man has never wavered. I am eternally grateful that I pursued my research and was not seduced by romantic women novelists who have concentrated only on his amorous adventures — and still do. That he indulged in a colourful love-life there is no question (the dukes owe him a debt of gratitude) but, by concentrating on this aspect of his character only, his sterling qualities and his brilliant brain have been almost ignored. It is mainly due to the great modern-day historian Sir Arthur Bryant that at last a true assessment of his qualities and achievements has emerged. It has been said that people are born with their dispositions but their characters are formed by circumstances, an axiom to which I heartily subscribe. It is from this angle that I am attempting to portray the man who was born to be king.

Security in early childhood has a lasting effect on one's life and, although the Prince of Wales enjoyed that security in his childhood, the rest of his fifty-five years could be termed the years of survival. That Charles became the man he was is evidence of his strength of character and, cynical though he may have been, he never became bitter or vindictive: a lesser man would have succumbed. Charles was the antithesis of his parents, the little French Queen Henrietta Maria and the rigidly moral, unbending Charles I, who was to die a Protestant martyr. The Prince of Wales was born into the most strait-laced and formal royal household in Europe. Both his parents were of small stature, while their son was to grow to manhood 'more than two yards high', with a swarthy complexion which earned him the title of 'The Black Boy'. Physically he resembled his maternal grandfather Henry IV of France, and his Stuart grandmother, the ill-fated Mary of Scots, was six feet tall.

The christening of the Prince of Wales was naturally a very grand affair, rather marred by the fact that His Grace of Canterbury was unable to officiate as he was 'inside' doing time. The Primate of All England had, when out shooting, killed a game-keeper instead of the buck at which he was aiming! As was usual in those days the baby Prince was given a household of his own with Sir William Cavendish, the Earl of Newcastle, as his Governor. In 1664 King Charles II created Cavendish Earl of Ogle and Duke of Newcastle upon Tyne in recognition of his loyalty to the Stuart cause. His mother was an Ogle of Bothal Castle near Morpeth. Northumbrians are great infiltrators. There is still in existence a touching letter from Queen Henrietta Maria to her infant son admonishing him after an adverse report of his royal charge had been received from his Governor. I feel the Queen's words are worth quoting in full.

> *'Charles, I am sorry that I must begin my first letter by chiding you, because I hear that you will not take physic.*
> *I hope it is only for the day, and that tomorrow you will*

do it, for if you will not I must come to you and make you take it, for it is for your health.'

Henrietta must have had strong maternal instincts, rarely exhibited in royalty in the seventeenth century. There are no records to tell us if the future king obeyed his mother's threats.

Children matured quickly in those days and at eight years of age the Prince of Wales was installed a Knight of the Garter, which is the senior English order of chivalry. Here again Northumberland encroaches, as legend has it that it was at Wark on the Tweed where Edward III was staying that the Order was created. The King was dancing with the Countess of Salisbury when she lost her garter. The knights burst into ribald mirth, much to His Majesty's annoyance. He picked up the garter with the point of his sword and in a resounding voice spoke the words which are now the motto of the Garter knights: 'Honi soit qui mal y pense', adding, 'Shortly you shall see that garter advanced to so high an honour and renown as to account yourselves happy to wear it.' Apocryphal or not, it is a good story.

The family of the King and Queen increased rapidly. Their second son, James, Duke of York, grew up to be an unpopular man (and an even worse sovereign); he provoked the famous remark made by Charles — 'They'll never kill me as long as you're alive, Jamie.' Five more children were to follow, the youngest, Minette, being born in the besieged city of Exeter during the Civil Wars. It was she whom her eldest brother loved more than any other human being. This love was reciprocated and Minette was to write to him in the years to come that she loved him more than life itself.

Henrietta Maria was anything but an adoring mother and was realistic in her opinion of her offspring and their looks to the point of harshness. When she saw her eldest son for the first time she remarked that he was the ugliest baby she had ever seen! Whether one agrees with Queen Henrietta or not, the ugly baby grew into a tall, graceful boy with a most beautiful speaking voice, more than his share of the Stuart charm and the most precious attribute anyone can possess — the ability to laugh at himself. Adulation to which royalty is subjected never appears to have gone to his head, though his creature comforts were many and his youth spent in beautiful surroundings. The King his father gathered together one of the most wonderful art collections in history, illustrated in the recent television series 'Royal Heritage'. Scattered and desecrated though these treasures were by the philistine Roundheads, many have been recovered and are to be seen in Her Majesty's collection, in art galleries and stately homes. Above all his royal homes, Windsor held pride of place in Charles' heart and did until the end of his life. There he could fish and hunt, play tennis and enjoy the outdoor life which was to stand him in good stead when he was a man on the run after the defeat at Worcester.

On the surface the life of the Prince of Wales seemed to be set fair, yet there were underground rumblings from those who opposed Charles I's despotic rule. The King believed firmly, one could say fanatically, in asserting the Divine Right of Kings. To him compromise was abhorrent and these views were encouraged, if encouragement they needed, by his unbending Catholic Queen. Young though he was, the boy Prince was aware that such policies were outmoded and, though unswerving in his loyalty to his King and father, he learnt that expediency is a valuable attribute in a ruler. This precept he carried out all through his life, both for the good of himself and his country.

In 1642 the storm broke, the Cavaliers and Roundheads divided the country and from then until 1649, with only a brief and superficial peace intervening, the country was torn apart by the Civil Wars. Young as they were, the Prince of Wales and the Duke of York saw action, saw the fortunes of their father ebb and flow, heard the dread name of Cromwell and met their soldier uncle, Rupert of the Rhine. The years of security and privilege were over, years of flight and exile lay ahead. The Parliamentarians delivered the death blow to the Royalist cause at Naseby, and the King was the prisoner of his subjects. The last great act of treachery was perpetrated by the traitor fiend Argyll, 'the man who sold his king for gold'. McCallum Mhor was living up to the evil reputation of his clan.

55

The Queen had escaped to France, to be followed years afterwards by her youngest child, Minette. Mary, the eldest daughter, was married to the Stadholder of the Netherlands. Princess Elizabeth and the Duke of Gloucester were at Syon House in the care of the Duke of Northumberland, who was a Parliamentarian. The King requested that his children be brought to St James Palace to bid him farewell. This request was granted and on Monday 29th January, the day before his execution, the children saw their father for the last time. Tears come to my eyes at the thought of that tragic farewell. Princess Elizabeth's grief was uncontrollable and those who witnessed it prophesied her early death. Sadly the prophecy was fulfilled. The fourteen-year-old girl was incarcerated in Carisbrooke Castle on the Isle of Wight, where she died, literally of a broken heart. Her brother, Henry of Gloucester, eventually reached France to join the court of his exiled mother where he died at the early age of twenty in Restoration Year.

Charles and James had fled to the Scillies and from there to Jersey. When I was in Jersey some years ago I had hoped to visit Elizabeth Castle where Charles spent some time: unfortunately the weather was too rough for the crossing of the causeway. At the time a friend expressed surprise that I hadn't attempted to swim out, as in those days I never gave in. I met an islander who told me with great pride that he was descended from Charles II. There is no evidence to disprove his statement! From Jersey Charles joined his sister Mary in the Netherlands and it was there, four days after the event, that the nineteen-year-old boy heard the news of his father's terrible death. The boy king broke down completely and wept for days. The thirtieth of January 1649 would be engraved on his heart forever.

England was a Commonwealth and Cromwell, though he might euphemistically describe himself as Lord Protector, was in fact a dictator. Scotland and the loyalty of the great Montrose remained the only hope. Unaware of Argyll's treachery, the young and inexperienced King believed the Campbell promise that, if he returned to Scotland and signed the Covenant, the country would support him and spare Montrose's life. Unhappily Charles believed the false Argyll and set sail for his

56

Scottish kingdom. Argyll moved swiftly and without trial the great Marquis was 'taken to the Watergate, hidebound with hempen span' and hanged as a common felon. By the time Charles reached the north-east coast of Scotland his most loyal friend and supporter was dead. Montrose had passed into history.

It was at Garmouth in Moray that the King landed. I was told when I went to Garmouth that he was carried ashore by a man named Mills, and that the exact spot was at Kingston. On the twenty-third of June 1650 the Solemn Deed and Covenant was signed in a house at Garmouth. Fond of Scotland though I am, my heart goes out to Charles during the time he spent among 'the unco guid'. Thundered at from the pulpit as he was, warned against the practices of the devil, harangued, threatened with the flames of hell were he to fall for the wiles and temptations of the infidels, it must have been enough to drive him into the arms of the devil. The smooth-tongued hypocrisy of Argyll and the men who hanged Montrose so disgusted him that he vowed never to return to his Scottish kingdom, and he never did.

It was August when he set out for the march south with high hopes of a royalist victory. By the west of England the armies marched until at last, on the third of September 1651, they came close to the city of Worcester. The King climbed the tower of the cathedral to view the formation of the Cromwellian forces with their background of the Severn. The Royalists were heavily outnumbered and the Parliamentarians, who had marched to battle to the tune of the Old Hundredth, familiar to us today as 'All People that on Earth do dwell', were seasoned troops. However much one may dislike Cromwell and his politics, there is no denying that he was a great general and knew how to lead men into battle. Well trained, well fed, the 'Ironsides' fought well and bravely and, courageous though the Cavaliers were, they were no match for the Roundheads . At three in the afternoon the Stuart cause was lost. Charles did his utmost to rally the stragglers but they had lost heart and the failure of General Leslie to commit himself and his men to action does not entitle him to battle honours.

Now for the uncrowned King it was escape if he could, as we all know he did, and one of the most extraordinary events in the lives of any of our monarchs was to pass into history and legend. When Charles endured the hardships and narrow escapes of a man on the run he would be in no condition to think that by his courage and endurance he was to strengthen his character and win the loyalty and admiration of the ordinary people he otherwise would never have known. The story of his hiding place in the oak tree at Boscobel has been recounted innumerable times, but it was only the beginning of his deeds of heroism and bravery in the six weeks he was a wanted man with a price on his head. I have beside me a newspaper cutting dating from the nineteen-sixties giving an account of the descendants of a family named Pendrell, whose ancestors provided the ladder by which Charles and his companion Captain Carlis climbed into the sanctuary of the famous oak. The Pendrells of 1651 were peasants who risked their lives to help their king. Mrs Pendrell washed his raw and blistered feet and gave him some workman's clean clothes and, most necessary of all, some food. For three days after Worcester the King had not eaten. Thirty years after he told Pepys he remembered the gnawing pangs of hunger! Sleep was another necessity and all night in their oak tree hide-out Charles lay in Captain Carlis's arms until the poor man's limbs were so numb he could scarcely move. It must have been a nerve-racking experience as the voices of Cromwell's men were heard talking beneath the shelter of the trees.

Charles had further darkened his complexion by rubbing soot over his face (some say it was walnut juice) but his height could not be disguised and his speech must have given him away, so different from that of the country folk who were helping him. He was recognized on several occasions but not a man betrayed him. Charles must have had nerves of steel as a Cromwellian soldier stopped him and said that they were still looking for that rogue Charles Stuart, to which Charles replied that he hoped the rogue would soon be caught and hanged!

The most outstanding episode which is rarely mentioned is the courage and resourcefulness of a young woman from

Staffordshire, Jane Lane. Perhaps the reason for Jane Lane's obscurity is the fact that there was no love affair between Jane and her 'servant', William Jackson. Jane Lane was the sister of Colonel Lane of Bentley Hall and an ardent Royalist. Before the battle of Worcester Jane had arranged to visit a friend near Bristol and had obtained a pass for herself and a man-servant. It was a heaven-sent opportunity to get the King out of the danger zone and the brave girl was eager to do all she could to assist in the escape. For some days, to quote, 'She carried the crown of England in her hands'. There were several narrow escapes on the journey. The man-servant was unable to saddle a horse, someone had always done it for him. He had no idea how to turn the spit for roasting meat, but with great presence of mind said that his family was so poor they never had meat and therefore he had never seen a spit. These are the little things which can make or mar any dangerous plan; this was to be so hundreds of years later with the Resistance workers who often gave away their identities by small mistakes.

Before the October day dawned when at last The Great Escape was a reality the wanderings of the king are somewhat confused. Many of the accounts vary; even his friends who helped him give different versions. What is factual is that as well as friends he met enemies who would willingly have taken blood money. By good fortune or, as his most loyal friend Father Huddleston would say, by the Grace of God he always managed to outwit those who would have played Judas Iscariot. Loyal and generous to his friends, tolerant of his enemies, Charles Stuart understood only too well the temptations and frailties that plague the human race. When he returned those who risked their lives for him were justly rewarded. Pensions are still being paid in 1981; some to descendants of those who played their parts in those six eventful weeks now living in Canada.

It is quite impossible in a chapter of this length to follow him step by step as he traced and retraced his way through the west country from one hiding place to another, from one disguise to another, yet how fascinating it would be actually to follow in his footsteps and re-live those episodes which not only made a man

59

but made a king. I have followed him to Shoreham where, on the fifteenth of October 1651, with his companion-in-arms Colonel Wilmot he clambered aboard the *Surprise*. Fair stood the wind for France, the King without a crown was free. It was to be nine long years until he stood on English soil again. The waiting was wearisome and disheartening but it was to end in triumph and in 1660 the King Came into His Own Again.

CHAPTER EIGHT

CHARLES II, PORTRAIT OF A MAN (Part II)

*Here out of the window it was a most pleasant sight to see
the City from one end to the other with glory about it, so
high was the light of the bonfires, and so thick round the
City, and the bells rang everywhere.*

Samuel Pepys

SO WROTE the indefatigable diarist Mr Pepys on the
twenty-first of February 1660. Eleven years of dictatorial and
puritanical rule were over. The Lord Protector, or Old Noll as
the Cavaliers called him, died in 1658 and was succeeded by his
ineffectual eldest son 'Poor Dick'. Making no attempt to rule
Richard Cromwell was ousted by Parliament and the army and
retired into obscurity, lamented by none. The Royalists' hour
had come and they were quick to seize their opportunity. North
of the Border General Monk was ready to march at the head of
an army which was to gain immortality as one of the famous
British Regiments, the Coldstream Guards. On the continent
the King was waiting for the summons. The years of wandering
from court to court on the continent, unwanted, an
embarrassment to his French relatives, penniless, scorned by
the foreign princesses who had no use for a king without a
crown, were coming to an end.

In May 1660 the summons came: the Glorious Restoration
was no longer a dream but a reality. A ship, the *Naseby*, hastily
renamed *The Royal Charles*, was ready. Charles was
accompanied by many who had shared his years of wandering
and amongst these the most dazzling of all was his beautiful
Aunt Elizabeth, Queen of Bohemia, the Winter Queen.
Shakespeare had written *The Tempest* in her honour. This
beautiful and gifted woman had drawn most of the crowned
heads of Europe to her exiled court, and was to retain her charm

well into old age. It is ironical that through the marriage of her daughter Sophia she became the grandmother of the German interloper George who succeeded the last of the Stuart dynasty, Queen Anne, and founded the House of Hanover in Britain. The Scots referred to him as 'the wee German Lairdie'.

All this was in the future when on the twenty-fifth of May *The Royal Charles* set sail for England. The weather was glorious and the sun shone on the white cliffs of Dover as the king stepped ashore on the crowded beach. The guns fired salutes from Dover Castle, the people cheered their almost hysterical welcome: Charles had come home. Some would say the King's first words when he landed were cynical. I would say they were realistic and that he was well aware of the fickleness of public approbation. 'Where are my enemies now?' asked the King as he surveyed the crowds. Everyone was asserting that he had always been a Cavalier, no Roundheads had ever existed. Well might the King ask where his erstwhile enemies were. People are always ready to change colours to the winning side. After the Second World War I never met a German, but one, who admitted to being a Nazi. It is a cliché but human nature does not change with the times. A contributory factor to the joy of the people was that the days of austerity imposed by Cromwell were over, the maypoles could come back to the village greens, the severe puritan clothes were discarded and dress, both for men and women, was once more colourful, one could describe it as flamboyant. The people could dance and sing again without fear of retribution. It was a natural reaction and understandably led to extremes.

As the King rode through the Kentish coutryside the blossom was in all its glory, the grass was green, the wayside flowers were in bloom. A new era had dawned. After many years of silence the bells of England's shrine of Canterbury rang out their welcome. The country folk lined the roads, cheering the King as he advanced towards his capital.

On the twenty-ninth of May, which was his thirtieth birthday, Charles drew rein at Blackheath and looked upon the London of his childhood again. Some years ago when I stood on the white cliffs I felt so near to that long ago month of May that I could picture it all and, as I followed the royal route to Canterbury, I too was one of the cheering crowd, so alive has this man become for me. His greatest appeal is his humanity. In a cruel age he urged moderation and clemency and, unusually, he loved animals. In many of the famous portraits of this most colourful of our monarchs, the spaniels which bear his name have a place of honour. What the corgis are to the Royal family today the spaniels were to Charles. He decreed that these endearing little dogs should have the privilege of free travel for all time. One wonders if British Rail would honour this edict! It would be an enlightening experience to test Sir Peter Parker's knowledge of history by arriving at King's Cross with a basketful of the King's favourite pets and demanding free travel!

Charles was a bachelor when he was crowned at Westminster in April 1661. The twenty-five years of his reign had begun. It was a reign of sharp contrasts, of extremes of popularity and unrest which changed with events; years when expediency was the only factor which stabilised the monarchy, when at times against his better judgement he was forced, as many have been since, to bow to the will of Parliament; to sign death warrants which he knew were merely for political gain and to display leniency to those who were ready at any opportune moment to bring about his downfall. Yet he never publicly displayed his feelings unless he felt the occasion justified the use of the royal prerogative. When the Royalists were thirsting for vengeance and were revelling in trials and executions, Charles exclaimed, 'Enough of this blood-letting, let us rule with mercy'. Only in the case of the regicides did he consider that the men who had brought his father to the block should pay the extreme penalty. Any son would have acted in the same manner had he been confronted with his father's murderers. One must remember, too, that a constitutional monarchy had not been established and the King was involved in politics as no sovereign is now. Lack of revenue was always with him: the country was poor and as always taxes were unpopular, and at times Parliament was uncontrollable, as it still can be today. The outstanding achievement of the reign was that he was able to remain in

63

power and, through the many storms, never to let the various Parliaments get the upper hand.

In the first part of this very personal interpretation of King Charles II, I was content to leave the struggles between King and Parliament to historians such as Sir Arthur Bryant and I will mention only briefly the names of some who played a vital part in state affairs. One who served him in exile and restoration was Edward Hyde, created first Earl of Clarendon. It was only when age and his overbearing qualities became an embarrassment that Charles was compelled to dismiss his old friend. Clarendon's daughter Anne was the first wife of James, Duke of York, and therefore Clarendon was the grandfather of Mary, the wife of Dutch William who was to rule as a joint sovereign, and of Anne as Queen Regnant, the last Stuart to rule Great Britain. The most famous group of men who held power in the government were Clifford, Arlington, Buckingham, Ashley and Lauderdale. The initials of their names earned them the title of the Cabal.

In the seventeenth century England was a rough, uncouth country: cruel sports and lack of humanity went hand in hand. The humour was bawdy, as the Restoration comedies testify, virtue was rare — the permissive society is not the discovery of the nineteen-sixties — but above all religious intolerance can be compared only with that practised in Northern Ireland today. I am an Anglican but I say that the persecution of those who adhered to the old faith was appalling. The King, outwardly an Anglican, wanted to leave the people to worship in their own way and stop the persecution. This did not please the extremists and many Jesuit priests suffered terrible deaths.

On the happier side the King was able to enrich and beautify London. It is to him that we owe gratitude for many gardens and the enchanting open space of St James' Park, where he walked freely and talked with his subjects. Royal walk-abouts are not a product of this age. He was the most accessible of our kings, even dining in public in Inigo Jones's Banqueting Hall at Whitehall. Science fascinated this forward-looking monarch and he was President of the Royal Society. Charles Stuart had great physical courage which was never more apparent than when London was burning. In 1666, the year after the Plague had decimated the population, the Great Fire raged. The King and the Duke of York rushed to the blazing inferno and, throwing off their wigs and velvet jackets, helped to fight the flames. It was their idea to contain the blaze by razing to the ground the adjacent streets which were not yet alight and so prevent the fire from spreading. This method is still adopted today when a large fire breaks out. Pomp and pageantry he loved (and so do I). The Life Guards and the Horse Guards (the Blues and Royals) were formed by Charles. Sir Christopher Wren would never have been able to build St Paul's as it is had King Charles not insisted that he must have freedom to modify the so-called 'warrant' design. It is amazing that Charles could devote so much time to affairs of state and yet indulge in so many other and diverse interests.

We are fortunate that two of the greatest diarists of all time, Pepys and Evelyn, were recording the momentous and the trivial affairs of this time. Pepys was the most avid gossip but he also had a brilliant career at the Admiralty, which people are inclined to forget and imagine his only concern was 'And so to bed'. When I was a child I kept a diary which was a monotonous recital of 'Got up, went to bed.' Not a treasure for posterity!

Racing was the King's relaxation: it is fitting that the sport is still termed the sport of kings. Newmarket was the headquarters of racing, as it is today. At that time there was a stallion standing at Newmarket named Old Rowley; the famous mile on the race course commemorates the stallion by name. In later life the King was often referred to as 'Old Rowley'. No explantion is necessary! The Rye House Plot, a plan to kill Charles and the Duke of York, failed only because a fire at Newmarket delayed the departure of the two brothers.

The time has come for me to embark on the more intimate side of His Majesty's life, his marriage and his love life. The bride chosen for the King was the Portuguese Princess, Catherine of Braganza, a Catholic, who was to bring as her dowry Bombay and Tangier and, more tangibly, a cargo of sugar and spices. In a television quiz programme in which I took part one question was, what was Catherine of Braganza's dowry? How thankful I was that I had studied the life of Charles II and could play my trump card. One wonders how much the little bride knew about her future husband's escapades. The Portuguese Court was incredibly strict; no unmarried lady would lie in a bed in which a man had slept! Catherine and her attendants must have reeled with shock when they came to Restoration England! In 1662 Catherine landed at Portsmouth and two people who had never even seen one another were married. There were two ceremonies, Anglican and Catholic, the latter in private. The King and Queen entered London by the river which has seen so much history. In spite of his infidelities the Queen was wildly in love with her husband. She accepted him for what he was and he, in his turn, treated her with the greatest respect and he demanded that his subjects (including his mistresses) should do the same. Had Catherine borne a living child the whole course of English history would have been changed.

Charles had been susceptible to women since an early age and he was to remain so all his life. Those who condemn him for his philanderings will be surprised to learn that when that most moral and strait-laced Sovereign Lady Queen Victoria was asked which of her royal ancestors she would most liked to have sat next to at dinner, her prompt reply was, 'Charles the Second'. I share Her Majesty's views! Burke's Peerage gives Charles fifteen illegitimate children while the Scottish Peerage goes one better and gives him sixteen! I have no intention of listing all the offspring.

Many of the aristocracy of this country can trace their origin to Charles and are proud to display the baton sinister. I quote the following extract: 'Baton Sinister. Arms of Dukes of Buccleuch, Grafton and St Albans, all of whom are descended from bastard sons of Charles II and use his arms debruised to denote their illegitimate descent.' The Buccleuch descent is from Monmouth, the child the King loved most of all his numerous 'family' and whose behaviour broke his father's heart. James Crofts as he was known until his marriage with the Buccleuch heiress, when he changed his name to Scott, was born while Charles was in exile. His mother was a Welsh girl of easy virtue whose name was Lucy Walter. After his father's death 'King' Monmouth led an ill-fated rebellion against his Uncle James II and paid the price with his life.

The least likeable of the ladies in Charles's seraglio was Barbara Villiers, whose husband's name was Palmer. He was created Lord Castlemaine to keep him quiet and went abroad, returning to discover that in his absence his family had greatly increased. Barbara was made a Duchess in her own right and became the mother of six bastards, three of whom were given dukedoms. Barbara was ambitious, ruthless, amoral as well as immoral and the greatest gold digger of all time. Why Charles tolerated her behaviour for so long is a mystery. She was constantly unfaithful to her royal lover but perhaps, like most men, Charles hated scenes and Barbara, Duchess of Cleveland, made scene-throwing a fine art.

The son who interests me most was Henry Fitz Roy, who married Arlington's daughter. This Henry became the first Duke of Grafton and made his home at Euston Hall in Suffolk. As everyone knows the name Fitzroy denotes the son of a king and in the case of Grafton the King ordained that it should be two words. I wish to make this clear as this form of the name is unusual.

Almost twenty years ago a stroke of fortune came my way, arranged by a friend. I was invited by the tenth Duke of Grafton to stay at Euston and see the Stuart relics. Not being familiar with the world of dukes it was with trepidation that I set out by way of Cheltenham (that is another story) and arrived at Thetford in the evening. I see by my copy of *The Royal Fitz Roys* by Bernard Falk (Hutchinson, 1950) that the date was 6th-7th December 1962 and the rough notes I made then recall a most stimulating experience. At the time I simply could not believe that I, Nancy Ridley, was staying in the house where Charles had spent some time and where he went through the mock marriage ceremony with his French mistress Louise de Kerouallé. I must admit I was rather overcome but His Grace assured me that Minette would look after me! Her portrait was hanging in my bedroom. My notes say: 'A proclamation in the

67

King's own handwriting conferring the Garter on Henry Fitz Roy. A nightshirt case used by the King, dated 1664 and embroidered with the Royal Arms. A portrait of Barbara by Sir Peter Lely.' The Duke and I agreed that she was a formidable looking lady. A miniature of the Black Boy (Charles II) by Samuel Cooper evokes vivid memories, as do those of Charles, Monmouth and Nell Gwynne. There were bleeding bowls, relics of the barbaric medical methods of those days and, to complete my tour of the house, I saw the wonderful collection of magnificent pictures of horses by Stubbs. When I signed the Visitors' Book the name above mine was that of Mr George Howard of Castle Howard in Yorkshire, now chairman of the Governors of the BBC. I was moving in high circles.

A psychiatrist looking through my notes would have me certified, as among the royal anecdotes appears 'The World of Susie Wong'! I must have seen the show earlier that year when in London and perhaps there was some connection of thought between Barbara and Susie. Susie Wong is forgotten but never Euston and the wonderful private contact with my favourite King. I freely admit that I have so often been granted private views and access to possessions which are not shown to the public that I hate being an ordinary visitor to a stately home. I am well on the way to being a history snob.

Of all the women with whom Charles had affairs the one who truly loved him for himself was the little cockney who sold oranges at Drury Lane, Mistress Nell Gwynne. She made him laugh when the cares of state wearied him and she was always herself, common, vulgar, with a dreadful cockney accent but, above all, she was honest. One day when driving in her carriage the crowds mistook her for her hated rival Louise. Nellie put her head out of the window and shouted, "You're wrong, I'm the Protestant whore."

There is a charming little house in Windsor where she lived when under the King's protection. Nellie had two sons by Charles, neither of whom had been given titles. Nellie was furious, especially as Barbara's sons were dukes. She hated Louise but she loathed the Castlemaine, once dressing in mourning to 'celebrate' the eclipse of the Villiers woman. There is a story that one afternoon the King called to drink a dish of tea and play with his two small sons. He had been visiting St Albans that day which may account for the consequence of the visit. Nellie called out to the older boy, 'Come here, you little bastard.' The King was shocked and told her not to use such words in front of the children. Nellie turned on him and said, 'Well, that's what he is, ain't he, until you give him a title.' And so the first Duke of St Albans was created. True or not, it is a typical Nellie gesture.

She received less than any of the mistresses in the way of money or honours, yet it was she who gave the idea to the King that he should found a hospital for old soldiers, the Chelsea Pensioners' Home. Every year Nellie is remembered by the Old and Bold on the anniversary of the Chelsea Hospital's foundation. One cannot imagine Barbara or Louise caring for anyone but themselves and the advancement of their own children. Louise grabbed the dukedom of Richmond for her son. When Charles in his last illness said to the Duke of York, 'Let not poor Nellie starve' it was a request which, to his credit, James honoured. Nellie was only thirty-seven when she died. Whenever I see a Chelsea Pensioner I think of her.

History has sadly neglected the only woman to our knowledge who said 'No' to the amorous King and retained his affection. Frances Stuart, or La Belle Stuart as she is better known, was a distant relation and a member of the Queen's household. She is dismissed by many writers as a baby-faced, golden-haired, blue-eyed, stupid girl who loved playing childish games. My opinion is that she was a clever, calculating young woman who played her games to her own advantage. Even when she suffered an attack of smallpox Charles visited her and on her recovery made her the prototype for the Britannia on our coinage. Frances eloped with the Duke of Richmond and Lennox (not to be confused with the son of Louise) and Charles forgave her. La Belle Stuart outlived her husband by thirty years and left instructions that land should be purchased in Scotland and given the nostalgic name of Lennoxlove: surely one of the most endearing names any house could have. Charles, like most of the Stuarts, was highly sexed yet at the same time enjoyed the company of intelligent women and, unlike the Hanoverians, he never abandoned his mistresses.

The human being he loved above all others was his sister Minette and he was to grieve all his life after her death at the age of twenty-seven. They met for the last time in 1670 when the infamous treaty of Dover was signed, a secret treaty by which, principally for monetary reasons, Charles committed himself to disreputable intrigues with the King of France without the knowledge of Parliament. Minette died a few days later after her return to France.

Though by our standards the King was still a young man, the hardships he had endured, the constant wrangles with Parliament and the strenuous outdoor life he led were taking their toll. That Monmouth should plot to overthrow his father shocked him grievously. His plans to build a palace at Winchester were never to be fulfilled. In the early part of 1685 he had a stroke. As he lay stricken in his great bed, did the memories of all he had endured and achieved rouse the dying man? Was he the boy again who rode to battle with his father; the man who trusted the traitor Campbell; the fugitive from Worcester; did they all pass through his mind? Those he had loved, his father and Minette, were they coming to take him home?

When he was conscious he asked that all his many clocks should be wound up and he apologised for taking so long a time a-dying. The details of that deathbed scene are horrifying. The room was crowded with people, it was airless, his doctors bled him constantly and applied blisters to his poor feet. His constitution could not survive these almost medieval tortures. All his sons but Monmouth were there with the little Queen to say farewell. Catherine knelt and asked his forgiveness. He whispered, 'It is I who should ask yours'. At last the room was cleared and Louise, Duchess of Portsmouth, brought to the bedside an old priest to receive Charles into the faith after which he had long hankered, the Church of Rome. The priest was Father Huddleston who had aided Charles after the defeat at Worcester. The wheel had turned full cycle. On the sixth of

February the best and most brilliant of the Stuart kings died in the Palace of Whitehall.

'The King is dead. Long live the King.' Many years afterwards his faithful attendant Bruce wrote, 'My good and gracious King and master, Charles the Second, and the best that ever reigned over us, died in peace and glory, and the Lord God have mercy on his soul.'

E

CHAPTER NINE

THE FORTY-FIVE

The ships of war
Have come ashore,
And landed Royal Charlie.

WHEN I STOOD on the beach at Eriskay on 'Prince Charlie's
Strand' I could scarcely believe that a childhood dream had at
last come true and my long journey in the Young Chevalier's
footsteps had begun. The rain was coming down in torrents but
nothing could dampen my ardour or my sympathy for the
Jacobite cause. I am sure that Queen Victoria would have
considered it presumptuous of a subject to express the same
views as Her Majesty's yet, with due respect, I share those
views. Had she been alive at the time of the rebellions of the '15
and the '45 she said she would have been a Jacobite, and so
would I. It is apparent that our present Queen admires the
House of Stuart: she is the first of her line to give her children
christian names borne by that dynasty. Today we have another
Prince Charlie who has inherited the charm, or charisma as it is
termed today, of his namesakes of long ago. One of Her
Majesty's race horses was called Doutelle, the name of the
vessel which brought 'Bonnie Charlie' from France to Scotland
on that July day in 1745 when he stepped on Scottish soil for the
first time. Above the strand grows a pink convolvulus said to
have been planted by him and which flowers only on this
Hebridean island. Those who have no interest in history
associate Eriskay with the Love Lilt only: I confess that this
'lilt' is not a favourite of mine, haunting though its melody is.

When the Prince landed he was accompanied by leading
Jacobites known to posterity as 'The Seven Men of Moidart'.
One of the Seven was the Marquis of Tulliebardine, the
Jacobite Duke William of Atholl, who was later to raise the

Standard at Glenfinnan. His designation of 'Jacobite' was to distinguish him from his Hanoverian brother Duke James. In the Forty-Five, brother fought against brother and father against son, and many husbands and wives were on different sides. Another brother of the Jacobite Duke William was Lord George Murray, who was to be made Captain General of the Jacobite forces. Other members of the Seven were two Macdonalds and Captain Francis Strickland of Sizergh, an Englishman, who died in Carlisle four days before the date of his execution, so robbing the hangman of his victim. Descendants of Francis Strickland still live at Sizergh Castle in the county that was once Westmorland and is now Cumbria. For seven hundred years Stricklands have lived at Sizergh: it is now National Trust property. The remaining three of the Men of Moidart were two Irishmen — Sheridan, who had been a tutor to the Prince, and Captain O'Sullivan — and George Kelly, a non juring parson.

The name of Bonnie Prince Charlie is so much associated with Scotland that many are inclined to forget he was not in the accepted sense of the word a Scotsman. His exiled father, the Old Chevalier, had spent many years of exile on the continent and his mother, Clementina Sobieska, was Polish. He was born in Rome and had not the Gaelic, as the Highlanders describe those who have no knowledge of their ancient language, and he must have spoken English with a slightly foreign accent.

Scotland is made up of two different races, mainly descendants of Picts and Celts north of the Highland Line and south of the Line the Lowlanders. An important element of the Forty-Five is often misrepresented: it was not a rising between English and Scots, it was Stuart versus Hanoverian, and half Scotland was against 'the yellow-haired laddie' while many Englishmen fought and died for him. I find this misconception most irritating and make a point of driving the fact home. It is almost impossible to avoid romanticising the Forty-Five: all the elements of romance formed the background of an episode in our history that was more akin to a Greek tragedy than the more imaginative writers would have us believe. The eagle that hovered over *Doutelle* was not the symbol of victory predicted

73

by Macdonald, it was to prove an omen of death and despair.

When the Prince and his few followers sailed from Eriskay they landed on the mainland of Scotland at Arisaig of the silver sands of Morar, immortalised in 'The Road to the Isles'. They spent the first night in the Highlands in a 'black' house, a croft roofed with turf and heather, most of which have disappeared now. The black houses had no chimneys, so the adjective was appropriate. Only a handful of clansmen were waiting for 'the man born to be king'. I have fallen under the spell of the Highlands and Islands and find it difficult to refrain from an over-dramatisation of the truth. As I write I can see the silver sands and almost feel the atmosphere of suspense and eagerness as Charlie and The Seven Men waited at Arisaig where *Doutelle* was anchored. Drama was enacted when young Clanranald drew his sword and declared, 'Though no other man in the Highlands draw a sword I am ready to die for you.' Thus the first regiment on behalf of the Prince was raised, that of Clanranald.

The scenery from Arisaig to Glenfinnan is magnificent in its grandeur: mountains and lochs, peaty burns and rivers tumbling through the glens on their way to Morar and the sea. There is no more magnificent scenery in the world than that of the Western Highlands. I have seen the Rockies and the Alps yet still 'my heart is Highland'. By sea, road and loch Charlie and his men reached Glenfinnan and on 19th August 1745, where the Macdonald Memorial stands today, Tulliebardine raised the Standard of James III, the King *de jure*. Few people gathered at Glenfinnan to watch the ceremony. Anxiously the Prince and his followers were waiting for the Clans to join them and were relieved beyond measure when at last they heard the skirl of the pipes and a pass through the mountains became ablaze with the tartan of the Camerons. The Gentle Lochiel, the finest of them all, had brought out his men for Charlie. The fiery cross had gone out and the Clans, with few exceptions, responded. The Macdonald of Armadale and the Macleods were noticeable absentees. Another absentee, who was as usual sitting on the fence, was Simon the Fox, the Chief of Clan Fraser or, as he termed himself, 'the Greatest Lord Lovat of

All'. Skulking in his own country The Fraser sent his son The Master of Lovat to represent him. This perfidy was to no purpose. Lord Lovat was to be the last Scotsman to die by the executioner's axe. After the debacle of Culloden Simon, who had remained in hiding, was found by the Redcoats hiding in a hollow tree and was taken to London. Turncoat and intriguer though he was, his spirit towards the end of his life and his wry sense of humour rouse one's admiration. After the death sentence had been passed on him in Westminster Hall Lovat was driven back to the Tower, sitting in his carriage with the sharp edge of the axe pointing towards him, as was the barbaric custom. Crowds lined the streets to watch the grisly spectacle and a cockney woman called out, 'You're going to have your head cut off, you ugly old Scotch dog.' Lovat poked his head out of the carriage window and shouted, 'You're right, you ugly old English bitch.'

With pride and a feeling of sadness I recall that the last Englishman to suffer this dreadful form of execution was a Northumbrian, Charles Radcliffe, the younger brother of 'Derwentwater's Bonnie Martyred Earl'. Charles had escaped from Newgate after the Fifteen but came home from exile to follow Charlie. Styling himself the fourth Earl, Charles was arrested on board ship lying off the Dogger Bank. He was tried for his part in the earlier rebellion and executed on the eighth of December 1746. Related through his mother to the Prince, Charles Radcliffe, like all his race, knew how to die.

Death was far from the minds of those who marched from Glenfinnan on that August day over two centuries ago. Without support from France, ill equipped and with little or no organisation, the Highlanders were spoiling for battle as the pipers led them through the glens. Over the dreaded Corrieyairack Pass, where the Great Montrose had made his epic march in the depths of winter of 1645, the clansmen, led by an inexperienced young man of twenty-five, turned southwards by Dalwhinnie and Dunkeld down by the Tummel and the banks of the Garry. Supporters, including Lord George Murray, joined them on the way and they entered Perth on the fourth of September. When I was in Perth the band of The

Black Watch was parading with pipes playing and drums beating; this famous Scottish Regiment was raised in 1725 to protect and keep peace in the Highlands. Their regimental tartan has no association with any clan. The Forty Twa' has the honour of having as their Colonel-in-Chief Her Majesty Queen Elizabeth the Queen Mother. Prince Charlie lodged in the Salutation Hotel, visiting Blair Atholl during his stay in the Fair City.

From Perth the army marched by Linlithgow to Stirling where its castle stands guardian over the Links of Forth. On the seventeenth of September Charles Edward Stuart looked upon the City of Edinburgh for the first time — the old city (Princes Street Gardens was a bog) with the great castle on its mighty rock towering above the maze of streets and wynds surrounded by the Flodden Wall.

Edinburgh was holding out for the Hanoverians: the Castle Garrison never surrendered. It was at the Netherbow that the Jacobite army entered the capital of Scotland. A coach had just passed through and the guards were in a drunken stupor when the Camerons, under the command of Lochiel, stormed their way in through the Gate uttering blood-curdling yells; and without a casualty Edinburgh surrendered. Lochiel had ordered his men not to use violence. During the entire campaign the Jacobite army carried out the rules which we would now describe as those of the Geneva Convention. It was the Hanoverians who were guilty of brutality and inhumanity.

On September the twenty-first the Prince's army routed the Hanoverians at the Battle of Prestonpans, which is a little south of Edinburgh. A man named Anderson guided the Prince's troops through the treacherous moss and surprised General Cope. 'Johnny' Cope is the only general in the history of the British Army who fled to Headquarters with the news of his own defeat. He galloped to Berwick upon Tweed to break the 'glad' tidings and inspired the jingle:

Hey, Johnny Cope, are ye waukin' yet,
Are your drums a-beatin' yet,
Hey, Johnny Cope, are ye waukin' yet
To gan' for the coals in the morning.

For about six weeks Prince Charlie had his 'finest hour', to borrow Sir Winston Churchill's famous phrase. All the Edinburgh ladies declared themselves dedicated to the Jacobite cause: they all wore the White Cockade when they attended receptions in the candle-lit gallery of Holyrood where Charles held his Court. In his Highland dress, with lace ruffles at throat and wrist, he was 'Bonnie Prince Charlie' of romance.

Flushed with victory the Jacobite army prepared to march on England and with their spirits high they said goodbye to Edinburgh Toon on the eighth of November. The Council's list of names reads like a Scottish history book, with the exception of the Irishmen who were stirring up as much jealousy and ill-feeling as they possible could, which was to bedevil the entire campaign, and quarrelling broke out among the Council members. I cannot resist recording the famous names of the Scottish nobles: the Duke of Perth, who was to die when carried on board the ship in which Charlie left Scotland for ever: Lords Lewis Gordon, George Murray, Elcho, Ogilvy, Pitsligo and Nairne, young Lochiel, young Clanranald, Keppoch, Glencoe, Lochgarry, Ardshiel, Gordon of Glenbucket — another 'roll of names'.

For the march into England the army divided into three columns, crossing the Border at different points. The Prince's column crossed the Border Esk near Canonbie in Dumfriesshire where he spent the night at the Riddings. (This was the farm whence Scottie came, the horse I wrote about in my first chapter and if a horse can be an inspiration, which I am sure it can, Scottie fired my interest in the Forty-Five.) Charles spent six weeks in England, three in the county of Cumberland (now Cumbria). The house where he stayed in the market town of Brampton has survived the march of 'progress' and is now a shoe shop. The house where his staff stayed has been demolished. The City of Carlisle surrendered without much opposition and the Duke of Perth led the army into Carlisle 'wi' a hundred pipers and a'. Whenever I am in Carlisle and walk along English Street, I look above the windows of Marks and Spencer which stands on the site of a house where Charlie stayed. At each end of the frontage are two inscribed tablets.

The words on the first one are 'Prince Charles Edward Stuart stayed here 1745' while the other bears the ominous words 'The Duke of Cumberland stayed here 1746'. The Mayor and Corporation of Carlisle came to Brampton and on bended knees handed over the keys of Carlisle to the Duke of Perth.

After much argument the decision was taken to march south by way of Penrith, Kendal and the wild Shap Fell and so into Lancashire, where the Jacobites hoped for support — a hope which did not materialise — and so to Manchester where they were given an enthusiastic reception. On the retreat they were booed and hissed at by the Mancunians, such is the fickleness of human nature. On December 4th they reached the outskirts of Derby. I have stood on Swarkston Bridge about six miles from the City where the Prince's contingent joined the forces of Lord George Murray and the rest of the army. I am told that Lord Exeter's house in Full Street, where the Prince stayed in Derby, is still standing but I cannot vouch for this.

The Intelligence Service of the Jacobite army must have been utterly useless. Had they but known it, Wade and Cumberland had been out-manoeuvred: Wade was at Wetherby and Cumberland at Lichfield, and the way to London was open. That very unlikeable character George II was packing his bags to return to his native Hanover, a departure which would have caused little regret. The Trained Bands were all drunk and if, and all history is an if, they had advanced instead of retreating a Stuart would be on the throne of this country today. Whether this would have been for the best in view of the deterioration of Charlie's character in later years is open to conjecture.

What really happened at Derby on Black Friday, 6th December, will never be known in detail. Charlie himself supported those who planned to advance but was over-ruled by those who counselled retreat. I would not venture to apportion blame to any one particular leader; they were jealous of one another, old rivalries had broken out and relations between the Prince and Lord George Murray were at breaking point. The final decision, unanimous or not, was made and the terrible retreat began. Instead of marching with his men as he had done

78

on the advance, the disappointed Prince rode in his coach. It was bitter winter weather, the roads were appalling, the last of the pitifully small number of cannon was bogged down at Sedbergh. They did not march over Shap, they struggled, and at Clifton, near Penrith, had a skirmish with the Redcoats. I have described the last 'battle' fought on English soil in *A Northumbrian at Large*. Carlisle was by-passed and the wretched garrison left to their fate. A very brave gentleman, Francis Townley from Burnley, was one of the victims to be hanged on Kennington Common. Once when I was speaking in Burnley I was taken to see Francis Townley's house, now owned by the local council. The house stands in beautifully kept grounds, an example of genuine care many councils should emulate.

The Border Esk was crossed again and though the songwriter would have us believe the troops danced for joy when they stood on Scottish ground again it was really to restore their circulation. The south-west of Scotland was hostile to the Stuarts: Galloway and The Stewartry had been a stronghold of the Covenanters. Glasgow was busy laying the foundations of an industrial city and had no time for a retreating army. It delights me to know that Charlie managed to get footwear for his weary men from some of the Glasgow merchants. It is interesting to read the household books kept by the Duke of Perth, every item of food was paid for. 4½ stone of 'bife' cost twelve shillings, 5 ducks three shillings and fourpence, 2 sheep fourteen shillings. Although all armies loot or, more euphemistically, 'win', this does not appear to have been so in the Forty-Five.

After a short stay at Bannockburn House, the opposing armies met at Falkirk. As in the case of the Battle of Sherrifmuir, history has never decided who were the victors! The Hanoverian General Hawley was so drunk he had to be hoisted onto his charger. I would dare to affirm that Falkirk was a Jacobite victory and should have been followed up while the Redcoats were still disorganised. Lord George Murray was having a great deal of trouble with the Highlanders who were deserting in large numbers. This is typically Highland: in battle there are no better or braver soldiers and it does not surprise me

79

that in the First World War the Germans called them 'the women of Hell', but when there is no action the Highlanders become restless and undisciplined and in the days of the Forty-Five they longed to return to their crofts and simply disappeared into the mountains.

Marching towards Inverness by the east coast route in winter was a terrible challenge of loyalty and endurance. Exhausted and hungry, it was a raggle-taggle army that encamped at Nairn and close behind them was a well fed, well disciplined one commanded by Prince William Augustus, Duke of Cumberland who well deserved the title of 'Butcher' posterity has bestowed upon him. How many times I have stood on dark Drumossie Moor I cannot remember but every pilgrimage I make to the scene of that massacre in April 1746 affects me as deeply as ever. The atmosphere is hushed and I feel almost personally involved.

The night before the slaughter began the Butcher had celebrated his birthday by giving his troops an extra tot of rum and double rations (he was the same age as his cousin, Charles Edward). Charlie's men had made a fruitless march to Nairn and back to Culloden where what sleep they had was in the parks surrounding Culloden House, wrapped in their plaids. Culloden House belonged to the Lord President, Duncan Forbes. When Culloden was fought the Lord President was in the Hebrides. A just and humane man, his presence might have controlled Cumberland's sadistic blood lust. On the morning of April 16th, five thousand cold and hungry men whose food consisted of 'pokes' of oatmeal, faced a well fed, well trained army of nine thousand Hanoverian troops. Many were German mercenaries, many were Scots. The largest Scottish contingent was composed of Campbells. The majority were regular soldiers drawn from crack regiments. On Charlie's side the Macdonalds, with their Highland pride, refused to charge as they had not been given the position they deemed to be their right since Bannockburn and were mown down.

Culloden was over in twenty-five minutes. Prince Charlie escaped on horseback before the last shot was fired and some managed to escape with him. The majority of his men lay dead and dying on the blood-soaked moor. Cumberland had given an order 'No quarter'. He wrote the infamous words on the back of the nine of diamonds, henceforth to be known as the curse of Scotland. He stood on a mound of stone when he gave the order and the stone bears his name to this day. Why the flower named Sweet William was called after him I cannot imagine, the Scots call it 'Stinking Billy' or 'Bloody Billy', either of which is much more appropriate. One Englishman, a young ensign, was ordered by the Butcher to shoot a wounded Fraser. The ensign replied, 'Sir, I am a soldier, not an assassin. You can accept my commission.' The officer's name was Wolfe. When General Wolfe lay dying on the Heights of Abraham above Quebec he was held in the arms of a Fraser who, some say, was the son of the man General Wolfe refused to murder on Culloden Moor.

The clansmen lie in the Long Graves; Macdonald, Fraser, Cameron — all the Jacobite clansmen are there. At some distance the English are buried and a stone inscription simply says: 'The Field of the English, they are buried here'. There is the Well of Weeping where the wounded dragged themselves to drink water and to bathe their dreadful wounds. Some wounded men were burnt alive in a cottage, now restored and used as a museum, a property of the National Trust for Scotland. The only consolation to mitigate this horrific page in our history is that the orders were given by a German. It will be obvious that I am not fond of the Germans. The curtain had come down on the Forty-Five. The Stuart defeat was the end of an auld sang but the campaign was lost before it started. By the Act of Settlement of 1701 only a Protestant could sit on the throne of Great Britain and Charlie was a Roman Catholic. For expediency he renounced the old faith for a time, but it was too late. A plain cairn commemorates the men who died for 'The King of the Highland hearts: Bonnie Prince Charlie'.

Many's the lad fought on that day,
Well the claymore could wield,
When the night fell, silently lay,
Dead on Culloden Field.

CHAPTER TEN

AFTER CULLODEN

Hills he trod were all his ain,
Bed beneath the birken tree.
The bush that hid him on the plain
None on earth can claim but he.

DURING THE fourteen months of Prince Charlie's ill-starred attempt to restore the Stuart monarchy in Britain the young Chevalier was a fugitive for some four months. After the Hanoverian victory at Culloden Charles Edward was a man on the run, as his ancestor Charles the Second had been after Worcester. The Government offered a reward of £30,000 for his capture.

Thirty-thousand pounds they gie,
Yet none there is that wad betray.

To the enternal credit of the Highlanders there is only one instance of an attempt to succumb to the lure of 'thirty pieces of silver'. This informer was none other than a 'Man of God'. The Reverend John Macaulay, grandfather of the notable historian, had discovered the Prince's whereabouts and was planning to pass on the information to the Chief of Clan Campbell. Mercifully it seemed that the vengeful god whom Macaulay worshipped had Jacobite sympathies and the infamous plot was foiled.

The first few days after Culloden were spent in confusion. The remnants of the army which had survived the slaughter gathered in Badenoch with the intention of pursuing the enemy Cumberland. Their leader, Lord George Murray, was still eager to strike a blow at the Butcher. This plan was abandoned when a message was received from the Prince commanding 'every man to seek his safety in the best way he can'. So many people erroneously believe that after Culloden Charlie escaped 'over the sea to Skye'. In fact it was to Benbecula that he fled. With Donald Macleod at the helm of a cockle-shell boat the little party landed in the Hebrides after a nightmare crossing from Arisaig where he had first set foot on the mainland of Scotland. Benbecula lies between South and North Uist, now joined by a causeway which was opened in 1960 by Her Majesty Queen Elizabeth the Queen Mother. When my pursuit of Charlie began I made the crossing from Lochboisdale in South Uist to Eriskay in a rowing boat: the heavens opened, waves were breaking over the bows and although I have never been on the run I feel that I should have some form of recognition for the hardships I have endured in following Prince Charlie!

To describe in detail the aimless wanderings on the islands would entail the writing of a whole book complete with maps. To those who wish to study this phase of Prince Charlie's wanderings I recommend Baron Porcelli's *The White Cockade* (Hutchinson). It is informative, well written and above all accurate. So many romances have been written without regard to accuracy that reality at times has been ignored. I love the Western Isles with an enduring love but the weather can be appalling and for hungry fugitives with their lives at risk it cannot have been romantic. I quote two extracts from contemporary letters which are illuminating. Lady Hugh Macdonald describes the Prince's clothes thus: 'His dress was then a tartan short coat and vest of the same got from Lady Clanranald, his nightcap linen all patched with soot drops, his shirt, hands, and face patched with the same, a short kilt, tartan hose, and Highland brogues, his upper coat being English cloth', a somewhat different picture than that portrayed in a ghastly film some years ago. Hollywood has a lot to answer for! The actor who played the part of Charlie bore no resemblance whatsoever to him and, though soaked to the skin and hiding in caves or sleeping out in the heather, he was always shaven, complete with buckled shoes, lace ruffles at throat and wrist and the famous 'lang yellow hair' combed and tied with a velvet ribbon!! His companions too were immaculate in tartans which had no connection with their clans. Everything was as large as life and twice as natural. Still, it was good box-office.

The reality was very different. The Redcoats were out in force, both by land and sea. Many of the Prince's most loyal friends had been captured and two of the most relentless 'hunters' were Scotsmen: Captains Scott and Ferguson. Sustained by brandy smuggled to them by friends (brandy cost one guinea an anker, which was ten gallons), the weary, unwashed, unshaven men at last reached South Uist. For a man who had enjoyed comfort, plentiful food and servants to attend to his needs, Prince Charlie's fortitude, good humour and courage are all the more commendable and surprising. He joked with the faithful few, never complained or showed signs of fear and was an inspiration to all who shared his hardships. In peril and adversity he displayed the qualities which truly made him 'King of the Highland Hearts'. The cave in which he hid near Lochboisdale is still there. One has to go by boat and scramble over the machair to reach it. The machair is the sandy land where coarse grass and masses of wildflowers grow close to the shores of the Atlantic.

It was in the June of 1746 that an unknown man brought news to the Prince that Captain Hugh Macdonald of Armadale had a plan which would enable the Prince to escape from South Uist, now alive with Redcoats. Captain Hugh Macdonald was not a Jacobite, he was commanding a company of Militia in Skye. Officially loyal to the Hanoverians, the Captain was a humane man and a secret admirer of the fugitive Prince. The plan which was propounded was destined to link Prince Charlie's name for all time with that of a young woman whose name was Flora Macdonald. Though only in each other's company for ten days, that brief encounter was to become immortal. Flora Macdonald is now a heroine of history, one of Scotland's most remarkable daughters, and Skye the most famous of the Isles. So often in life one says, 'I'll never forget the visit' to places one has always wished to see, yet how often one forgets. I can say categorically that the first time I saw the Cuillins is one of the most unforgettable experiences of my life; following Charlie gave me the opportunity to see some of the most glorious scenery in the world. The sun was shining when I crossed from Mallaig to Armadale, the sea studded with purple islands was as blue as the Mediterranean and the gigantic rugged peaks of the Cuillins formed a theatrical background. At long last I had come 'over the sea to Skye'. Making Portree my headquarters, my thoughts were with Charlie and Flora.

Flora Macdonald, the step-daughter of Captain Hugh, was keeping house for her brothers at Milton: now only the foundations of the house are to be seen. On that June evening long ago when the sun was setting over the archipelago, one of her brothers came into the house, excited and almost speechless. He managed to ask his sister if she would give refuge to a man who was on the run from Culloden. At first Flora was hesitant, reminding her brother of the consequences such an action would entail. As she was talking a tall, dishevelled young man came into the room and bending over the young woman's hand he told her who he was. From then onwards this courageous girl never wavered. She fed the royal fugitive and gave her word that she would do everything within her power to help him. Without the connivance of her step-father the historic voyage could not have been accomplished, for it was he who issued the passes for Flora and Prince Charlie. Reliable clansmen were found to take them to Skye. The waiting and suspense must have been an intolerable strain. Spies were everywhere yet, in spite of the dangerous situation, a boat was found. The Prince was to assume the role of maid to Flora. The 'maid' was described as Betty Burke, an Irishwoman (this nationality was chosen to account for his strange accent). Suitable clothes were found for 'Betty Burke', who had to be restrained from smoking a pipe and taking such long strides. The disguise was provided by Lady Macdonald of Nunton, wife of The Clanranald.

It was a stormy night when the famous voyage began. On the 29th June they set sail from Benbecula. There are conflicting accounts of the number and names of the crew and as their identities cannot be established I can only say with certainty that the men who manned the boat were risking their lives, and their loyalty was absolute.

85

Speed, bonnie boat, like a bird on the wing,
Onward the sailors cry,
Carry the lad that's born to be king,
Over the sea to Skye.

A legend had been born, a legend that will never die. It was a rough crossing over the Little Minch, so wild and rough that Flora lay on the bottom of the boat with her Prince attempting to protect her from the wind and the waves. The Prince always treated her with the greatest respect, bowing to her whenever they met, a courtesy he had to abandon when they encountered strangers. I have stood on the spot at Waternish in the northern corner of Skye where they landed. The Militia were encamped so near that the fugitives could see the fires burning.

So many members of the Clan Macdonald assisted Flora in her dangerous mission that there is some difficulty identifying those who were closely involved. Upon landing on Skye the original plan was to take refuge in Monkstadt House, the home of Sir Alexander Macdonald, the Clan Chief, and his wife Margaret. This was to prove too dangerous. Although Lady Margaret was a Jacobite her husband was officially a Hanoverian and was at that time visiting the Duke of Cumberland on the mainland at Fort Augustus. Fortunately for Flora, Alexander Macdonald, factor to Sir Alexander, was visiting Monkstadt when she arrived asking for help and readily offered to provide shelter for the fugitives in his own house at Kingsburgh.

At Kingsburgh for the first time for weeks the Prince slept in clean sheets. These sheets were preserved and some say were used as Flora Macdonald's winding sheets. Before going to his bed Mrs Macdonald, being a practical woman, gave her Prince a supper of 'roasted eggs, collops (slices of minced meat), bread, butter and beer and a pipe of tobacco. In Mrs Macdonald's case it can be authenticated that she did possess a lock of the Prince's hair, which Flora cut at his request as a keepsake for his courageous hostess. Were all the locks of hair one is shown in Scottish castles and great houses genuine, Charlie would have been bald when he left Scotland! The same applies to the pieces of tartan reputed to have come from the plaid he wore at Culloden: the plaid must have been big enough to cover Drumossie Moor. I cannot refrain from quoting a verse of 'The Auld Hoose' which is one of my favourite Jacobite songs.

> 'The wild rose and the jasmine
> That sheltered Scotland's heir,
> And clipped a lock wi' her ain hand
> From his lang yellow hair'.

The countless songs about the Forty-Five were written long after Charlie and Flora were dust. The most famous is 'The Skye Boat Song', sung the world over.

The presence of the Militia made it imperative that the journey to Portree was made as quickly as possible and so, with Flora on horseback and her 'maid' striding along beside her, they set out on the eight mile journey. Again there are conflicting accounts of exactly when they left Kingsburgh House, who accompanied them, what befell them on the way, was Charlie part of the time in Highland dress and so on. The relevant factor is that they did reach the capital of Skye and stayed in the Royal Hotel which was and still is an inn. It was there that Prince Charles Edward Stuart and Flora Macdonald parted, never to meet again. The truth may disappoint the romantically minded but there was never a love affair between them. How could there be? There is no time for dalliance when lives are at stake. That they were attracted to one another is more than likely: he was a Prince, young and good-looking, she was an attractive young woman and they shared the most dangerous situations. Had I been in Flora's position I would have fallen for Charlie in a big way and I well believe that when she was dying his was one of the last names she spoke. She thought of him in her heart for ever as 'Young Charlie'. When they parted at Portree her present from the Prince was a snuff-box and she, practical as always, gave him clean shirts, a cold ham, whisky, brandy and sugar. The famous journey was history already, their futures were a different story.

Flora was to be a prisoner in the Tower for the part she had taken in protecting the man with £30,000 on his head. When she was released she made a slow journey home to Skye, spending some time in Edinburgh. Her life was to be a happier one than that of Charlie. She married her cousin Allan Macdonald, a tacksman, and they emigrated to America, where she brought up her family. I hope to write in a further chapter how I chanced upon an episode in her life when I was in America. She was one of the few involved in the Forty-Five who came home again. Home to Flora was Skye and there she spent her last years near Flodigarry and was to have the doubtful pleasure of meeting Johnson and Boswell. I use the word doubtful, as these two inveterate travellers never seem to have enjoyed or approved of what they saw! In 1790 the heroine of the Forty-Five died at Kingsburgh House and is buried at Kilmuir where her descendants have erected a memorial.

There is a magnificent memorial to her at Inverness Castle. She is standing on a plinth looking westwards to the Isles.

> *Though the waves leap, soft shall ye sleep,*
> *Ocean a royal bed,*
> *Rocked in the deep, Flora will keep*
> *Watch by your weary head.*

Flora Macdonald did more than 'watch by his weary head', she succeeded in helping her Prince to escape. Without her assistance it is doubtful if he would have evaded his enemies. Her name is enshrined in the history of Scotland for all time.

Charlie was to suffer many hardships and narrow escapes before he left Scotland for ever. From Skye he crossed to the island of Raasay, then again to Skye, eventually reaching the mainland on the 6th July where he and his staunch followers lay for three nights in the open air. From now onwards the situation became even more desperate. Captain Ferguson had done his worst, many of the homes of men who fought at Culloden were burnt to the ground and the avenging armies of Butcher Cumberland were hunting every glen and mountain side. The Prince took refuge in a cave for many weary and hungry days. At times the enemy was so close he could hear the soldiers talking. Camerons and Macdonalds, to mention only two famous names, suffered with their Prince and followed him to the end.

I have shared one of Prince Charlie's many sufferings, bitten to death by the diabolical midges which abound in summertime in the Western Highlands. Charlie had no kindly chemist's shop to go to, as I had, to ask for lotion to alleviate my sufferings. I have come to the conclusion that these blood-sucking insects are of Hanoverian origin: they must have known I was a Jacobite! Those who describe Charlie as 'the Prince in the Heather' can never have suffered 'the Hell in the Heather'. I have described in my book *A Northumbrian at Large* some of the experiences I have survived for my allegiance to the Jacobite cause.

The loyalty of the Highlanders to Prince Charlie was literally such that it was live or die for Charlie. The Redcoats captured a Mackenzie who so closely resembled the Prince that his captors were convinced they had run him to earth. The Mackenzie claimed that he was indeed the hunted Prince, thus giving the genuine man time to get away. The Redcoats shot Mackenzie down in Glenmoriston and the spot can be seen today. In early September refuge was taken in the famous Cluny's Cave in Benalder, on the face of a mountain. Seven men in all were hidden in the 'Cage': Cluny was a Macpherson and faithful to the lost cause. The fugitives still had a hundred dangerous miles to travel to reach the coast, it was impossible to live off the land as the enemies had plundered and burnt everything in sight yet somehow bannocks, milk and brandy were brought to them by friends. On one occasion a cow was slaughtered and for once they were well fed.

On the eighteenth of September they saw the coastline and, lying offshore, the two French ships that were to take them into exile. Charles bade farewell to those who stayed behind. Many of them later paid for their loyalty with their lives. When the Prince boarded *Prince de Conti* twenty-three of his officers sailed with him, one of whom was the Gentle Lochiel. A hundred others also left their homeland: they were proscribed men who could never return to their own country. So *Prince de Conti* and *L'Heureux* sailed for France. The Forty-Five sealed the fate of the House of Stuart, and any hope of another attempt was finally crushed when Charlie's only brother Henry accepted a Cardinal's hat.

Bonnie Charlie's noo' awa',
Safely o'er the friendly main.
Mony a heart will break in twa',
Should he ne'er come back again.
Better loo'ed ye canna be,
Will ye no come back again.

A lament for Charlie, a lament for Culloden.

As I have not mentioned many of those who followed the Prince individually I am adding a list of some of the Clans and Regiments that fought at Culloden.

The Atholl Brigade. Lochiel's. Chisholm of Strathglass's. Earl of Cromartie's (Mckenzie's). Farquharson of Monaltrie's. Lord Lewis Gordon's. Gordon of Glenbucket's. Grant's of Glenmoriston and Glenurquhart. Lord Lovat's. MacDonell of Barrisdale's. MacDonald of Clanranald's. MacDonald of Glencoe. MacDonell of Glengarry's. MacDonald of Keppoch's. MacGregor's. Lady MacKintosh's. MacKinnon's. MacLachlan's. MacLaren's. MacLean's. MacPherson's. Lord Ogilvy's Regiment. Duke of Perth's. Robertson of Struan's. Appin Stewart's. Roy Stewart's. Lord John Drummond's. Pitsligo's Horse (the remnants of which fought a dismounted action). The Manchester Regiment and a handful of Irish and French.

I have no intention of writing about the years that lay ahead for Charles Edward. I never write about places I have not seen and although I have been in France and Italy I have never been to Rome. His life was not a happy one. Had it not been for the care and affection given him by his illegitimate daughter Charlotte towards the end of his life, he would have been alone and unloved. Charlotte was the baby born to Charles and Clementina Walkinshaw who nursed him at Bannockburn House after the battle of Falkirk. Charles created Charlotte Duchess of Albany.

I refuse to join that band of writers, now so fashionable, who denigrate and destroy any brave or heroic action which has caught the imagination of those who come after. That Charlie drank heavily there is no doubt. The eighteenth century was the age of 'the three bottle man' and who can blame 'the man born to be king' that he found solace for disappointment, exile and an unfortunate marriage in over-indulgence. The 'holier than thou' brigade should remember not only that 'there but for the grace of God go I', but read and reflect on the words of the first verse of the thirteenth chapter of Corinthians: 'Though I speak with the tongues of men and of angels, and have not charity, I am become as sounding brass or a tinkling cymbal'. At the age of sixty-eight Prince Charlie died at Frascati and is buried in St Peter's, Rome. Whatever his faults, he will always remain Bonnie Prince Charlie.

CHAPTER ELEVEN

NANCY IN THE NEW WORLD. PART I: CANADA, BRITISH COLUMBIA

I have no doubt at all the Devil grins,
As seas of ink I scatter;
Ye Gods, forgive my 'literary' sins —
The other kind don't matter.

R. W. *Service.*

MY INTEREST in Canada began when I was introduced to the poetry of Robert Service. I must have been what is now described as a teenager when I first discovered *Rhymes of A Rolling Stone* and *Songs of a Sourdough*, the name given to an old timer (gold miner) in Alaska. I cannot understand now why this type of verse appealed to me so much. Yet appeal it did and I used to reel off poem after poem, not having the remotest idea what they were about. Robert Service was an Englishman, born in 1874, who emigrated to Vancouver Island. That one day I should visit the Island and see a memorial to him never occurred to me and that his poetry is largely about the Yukon and the Gold Rush did not strike me as incongruous! Service died in 1952, twenty-two years before I achieved an ambition and spent three weeks in the country colonised by the British in 1759. General Wolfe, who had fought for the Hanoverians at Culloden, was to die on the Heights of Abraham in the hour of victory over the French. A statue of Wolfe stands at Westerham in Kent, close to the home of another great Englishman, Sir Winston Churchill, whose house at Chartwell is now preserved for the nation.

The decision to visit Canada came about in an altogether unexpected way. I received a letter from a Canadian solicitor asking for proof that I was the niece of the deceased owner of an oil well! I was able to prove that this 'tycoon' was indeed an

92

uncle, who had always been regarded as a rolling stone and who held extreme political, I would go as far as to say subversive, views. I was quite willing to overlook Uncle Charlie's failings if I were to be an heiress. For days I lived in a state of euphoria, only brought to earth by the deflating news that I was to receive the equivalent of £20 a year for the next thirty years, tax deducted at source! On the strength of my inherited wealth I determined to go to Vancouver Island, named after a Captain Vancouver who circumnavigated it in 1792-94, and stay with relations. I had met only one of these relations and that was for a brief period during World War II when he was serving in the Canadian army and was one of the many who took part in the Rhine crossing.

To the majority of people today a flight to Canada is nothing: to me it was a great adventure. I loathe and detest flying and behave like a lunatic when I am airborne. I never trust the pilot and my imagination conjures up the most terrible disasters. I once read that the safest part of a plane is the loo, but one cannot spend all those dreadful hours in the loo with irate and desperate passengers hammering at the door. I tried this refuge on a short flight from Copenhagen to Alberg and made myself extremely unpopular. On the flight from Heathrow to Vancouver I was fortunate enough to sit beside a couple from Ponteland who had recognised me on the flight from Woolsington — Newcastle airport — to Heathrow. By a coincidence we returned on the same plane and I am forever indebted to them for their forbearance and kindness. My friends left me at Vancouver Airport and I made the short flight to Victoria alone. I had no idea what my cousins looked like and I passed and re-passed groups of people waiting for friends. Eventually only one group was left and I made a timid approach to ask if they were meeting Nancy Ridley. 'Yes,' said one, 'but we are looking for someone very smart and English-looking.' Words for once failed me!

It was night and the drive from Victoria to Duncan (the latter best seen in the dark) was enchanting. The lights were blazing on the mainland, the night air was warm, the stars were bright and I could make out numerous totem posts by the roadside.

93

Although I kept a diary I have no intention of relating day by day the events and journeys we made. A diary is of interest only to the writer and is a deadly bore for a reader. I remember suffering terribly from jet-lag and spending most of the first day in bed. In the late afternoon we went for a drive and a cousin remarked casually as we passed a granite (?) memorial that it had been erected to the memory of a poet named Robert Service of whom I would never have heard!

I found it difficult to understand the strong accent of the West and must often have given the impression of being slightly vacant. Disappointingly for me 'my' Canadians had no interest in the history of their country and I had to curb my anecdotes, which I had memorised at great length before leaving home, otherwise I was going to sound like a school marm, a patronising Englishwoman, though obviously I was not the type regarded as such! I am not worried about the opinions I am expressing as none of the Duncan cousins were readers and are never likely to read my literary efforts. When one of my cousins subsequently visited me in England Nancy Ridley's epics were never mentioned. Before leaving, my cousin went to Newcastle to find some books about England, returning to Wylam with a copy of Burns' poetry, which none of them would be able to understand, it takes me all my time with some of the Ayrshire dialect, and Palgrave's Golden Treasury. Thus was the Ridley pride trampled in the dust.

One memorable day was our picnic to Torfino on the Pacific coast. Canadian ideas of distance are very different from ours: in that one day we covered more miles than there are from Wylam to London and back. There was a short stop by the Kennedy river, near a forest where the height of the trees was so terrific that it was named the Cathedral, and eventually we reached Torfino which, I admit, I found most disappointing. The sand was dull and drab and littered with hideous caravanettes. On the way back we called to see yet another cousin in Port Alberni and then, more dead than alive, we reached Duncan and bed. Possibly I am not being fair about this part of my visit and had I been with more congenial company my impressions would have been very different. That part was yet to come.

Before leaving England I had arranged, through The English Speaking Union, to give a couple of historical talks in Victoria and Vancouver. I had hoped that my cousins might have been able to make some contacts for me but they did not belong to that kind of world. I wish to make it absolutely clear that I received no fee for either of my talks and so explode the theory that I was making money out of my holiday. Yet I am glad I did accept these speaking engagements as one of them proved to be the highlight of my Canadian adventure and showed me a completely different side of Canadian life.

My first talk was in Victoria, which is one of the most beautiful cities I have ever seen. The atmosphere is so British that I felt I was living in the reign of Edward VII, not that of Elizabeth II. It gives the impression of the days when Britain was an Empire: the matriarchal figure of Queen Victoria proudly surveys the city which bears her name. The world-famous hotel, The Empress, recalls the days of the Empire on which the sun never set, the Union Jack flies side by side with the Maple Leaf, while a carillon of bells peal forth 'God Save the Queen' at regular intervals. I was in my element, and gave probably the best talk I have ever given in the Oak Bay Hotel. As it was September, the Fall was at its most glorious, the sea was sparkling and the hotel might have been in pre-war England. The men all wore dinner jackets, with the exception of the inevitable Scotsman wearing Highland evening dress. My cousin, who had been invited to dinner and to hear her famous relative, thought it all very 'stuffed shirt'. Her remark emphasises the different strata of Canadian society. It is not, as Canadians would have us believe, classless; it is class ridden and everyone has a grandmother who came from Skye! The Clearances have nothing on the exodus of grandmothers from the misty island!

The three days I spent in Victoria were three of the happiest of my visit. Cousin Charlie was a sheer delight, perhaps I found him so because we had similar tastes. Sadly this nicest of all my cousins died shortly after I came home. I was taken to see a very old house, Port Ellice, built in 1861, very modern by

Northumbrian standards but ancient to the Canadians. The brochure describes it as 'Amazing Haunted Ancestral Home of the O'Reillys', Ireland at least was a change from Skye. The brochure becomes more and more lyrical and asks the visitor to 'come and see Her Majesty Queen Victoria's personal signature and other Reigning Kings and Queens of England'. 'Captain Scott the famous Arctic explorer frequently escorted an O'Reilly daughter to social functions . . .' Port Ellice House has now been taken over by the Canadian Government and is preserved as an ancient monument. The Empress Hotel is unique, I felt more British than I do at home. Portraits of the Governors General line the long entrance hall walls: 'Radical Jack' (a Lambton from County Durham) is there and John Buchan (Lord Tweedsmuir), a Borderer, caught my eye at once. It was all so dignified and ladies having tea wore hats and gloves. As a complete contrast we went to a coastal fort on the curiously named Point No Point where it was rumoured Japanese ships were seen on the horizon after Pearl Harbour. Another day was spent in the famous Butchart Gardens, a paradise of flowers covering acres of what was once a quarry. All my memories of Victoria are happy, there was none of the bitterness, at least I didn't hear any, which I heard in other parts of the Island against the French influence and the Indian 'trash'. I became so exasperated one day that I said I might as well be in Northern Ireland. I badly wanted a china Canada goose and we tramped all over the city looking for one without success. After Cousin Charlie's death his widow sent me a brass goose which has pride of place among by souvenirs.

My next speaking date was in Vancouver, a city which, apart from the beautiful residential area where I stayed, did not impress me. There is a huge Chinese population and hideous skyscrapers dominate the dwarf-like streets below. My hosts in Vancouver were Australian and extremely kind. There was one snag — a cat named Oscar. As everyone knows I adore cats, but Oscar was not one of my favourites. He had a bedroom in the basement next to mine (he even had a name plate on the door) and Oscar decided to talk at the top of his penetrating Siamese voice all night. As our trip to the Rockies was to start next day I did not appreciate Oscar's vocal efforts. I did not give of my best in Vancouver. My audience was more cosmopolitan and less responsive than that in Victoria and the surroundings were drab in the extreme. That evening has left very little impression on me as opposed to the Rockies which most certainly did. This would become a guide book if I followed our journey in detail and so I will concentrate on what, for me, were the delights and the sheer hell of the many miles between Vancouver and Jasper which, of course, we had to do in stages.

I loved the first part of the journey through ranch country which I think my cousins called 'sage bush' country but, as I have already said, the heavy accent was sometimes unintelligible. Thousands of Hereford cattle were grazing on the ranches which we left behind at Kamloops. We spent our nights in self-catering motels and I have never eaten so much Kentucky chicken, nor do I belive they all came from Kentucky! One night we were desperate for accommodation and were directed to a somewhat dubious-looking district. At the hotel we were greeted by a very large lady who resembled Bloody Mary in *South Pacific* and wondered what horrors lay in store. We need not have worried. The rooms were clean and most attractive and there were flowers everywhere.

Had I known what lay before me in the Fraser Canyon and Roger's Pass I think I would have stayed with Bloody Mary. Sixty miles of hell through what the guide book comfortingly labels the Valley of Death! It was a case of canyon to the left of us, mountain to the right of us, below us the Thomson and Fraser Rivers and on the narrow track countless memorials to the men and mules who lost their lives when the road and the railway were hewn and blasted through the rock. In the worst parts we were led by a pilot car. The very thought of that test of endurance, and the knowledge that the return journey had to be made, still fills me with horror. The building of the Canadian Pacific Railway, and the National Railway, is one of the greatest feats of engineering man has ever achieved. I was fortunate enough to see a train doing a figure eight as it made its serpent-like way through the endless tunnels, the engine emerging while the rear of the train had still to enter the tunnel.

That was beside the Great Divide which is a watershed and where the provinces of British Columbia and Alberta meet. As we picnicked some whisky jays decided to join us and apart from some racoons they were the only wildlife I saw. Every day I was told I would see a bear — signs to beware of them were everywhere. I concluded that as the tourist season was over the bears had collected their honey and gone to ground. To appease me I was given a toy bear.

To me the Canadian Rockies were and are a world apart. Their majesty and dramatic beauty are quite beyond my powers of description. The atmosphere is so astonishingly clear as the great peaks tower over the valleys and gorges. With their snow-covered summits in the bright sunlight, the wealth of wild flowers in their foothills and the shimmering lakes they gave the impression that man here is of little importance, overshadowed by this colossus of nature. Mount Robson rises to 12,000 feet: the name intrigued me as one of the chief 'graynes' or clans of North Tyne in my own Northumberland are the Robsons. Some North Tyne emigrant must have given his name to the highest mountain in the Canadian range. The immortal memory of Edith Cavell is commemorated in the name of another. Lake Louise, with which I fell in love, was named after a daughter of Her Imperial Majesty, Queen Victoria, while the most lovely town in all the range of mountains, Banff, has obviously taken its name from that far north-eastern county of Scotland. Banff and the hotel at Lake Louise are sophisticated in comparison with most Candian towns and hotels of the West.

Jasper with its National Park I found extremely uninteresting. The town is a railway junction and has a faintly industrialised look. We spent a night in a log cabin near Jasper where we kept a log fire blazing as the nights are extremely cold. The bed, like most of those I encountered, was hard and uncomfortable. I would call Canadian beds 'rocky'. On our way back we saw a lone Mountie riding the range. One Mountie was the total score, which was something of an anti-climax after seeing them in the Coronation procession of 1953 and at the Edinburgh Tattoo. Mounties and bears were thin on the ground! I was impressed by the constant patrolling of the Trans-Canada Highway by the equivalent of our R.S.P.C.A.; we saw a number of their blue vans. Had it not been for the horror of the Fraser Canyon I loved my all-too-short stay in some of the most breathtaking scenery I have ever seen. Like the Americans, the Canadians revel in whistle-stop tours whilst I enjoy lingering and learning the history of places. Speed and the Almighty Dollar are the be-all and end-all of both countries. It was a Sunday when we embarked at Vancouver to cross to the Island. The bars were all closed and there was very little to eat and we still had a long drive to Duncan when we disembarked.

It is impossible in three short weeks to assess a country: one can only voice personal opinions and the country is so vast one would have to spend a great deal of time travelling from east to west to understand the many different ways of life. My impression was that Canada shares many of our problems, unemployment is endemic, strikes are frequent and it is not all the land of milk and honey one is led to believe. There is a certain amount of hostility towards Britain and I was so furious to hear our Royal Family derided, especially criticism of Her Majesty the Queen Mother, that I could not allow it to pass without comment. A great many of the settlers are of mid-European origin which results in a confusion of loyalties. In western Canada there appeared to me to be a very small middle-class, very upper-crust or working class predominated, and America has a strong influence in business and commerce. The less I say about television in either country the better! I am glad that I have been there, but to one of my traditional outlook and intense loyalty to the British throne it is not for me (excepting, of course, Victoria). I am inclined to agree with my mother's opinion that many misfits left their homeland for 'God's own country' and in her words 'they were no loss'. I realise that my outlook is insular and many people will howl me down for airing my prejudices. One compensation about growing old, and they are few, is that one has the courage to say what one thinks and to hell with other people's criticism.

I am ending this outburst with a legend that appealed to me greatly and it is surprisingly traditional to discover in such a young country.

The Dogwood

*There is a legend that at the time of the crucifixion the
dogwood had been the size of the oak and other forest
trees, so firm and strong it was chosen as the timber for the
cross. To be used for such a cruel purpose greatly distressed
the tree and Jesus, nailed upon it, sensed this. In his gentle
compassion for all sorrow and suffering he said to it,
'Because of your regret and pity for My suffering, never
again shall the dogwood grow large enough to be used for
a cross. Henceforth it shall be slender and twisted and its
blossoms in the form of a cross. At the outer edge of each
petal shall be nail prints brown with rust and stained with
red and in the centre of the flower shall be a crown of
thorns, and all who see shall remember.'*

CHAPTER TWELVE

NANCY IN THE NEW WORLD. PART II: THE UNITED STATES OF AMERICA

... and that government of the people,
by the people, and for the people,
shall not perish from the earth.
Abraham Lincoln, 19th November 1863.
Last lines of the famous
Gettysburg Address.

MY FIRST BOOK, *Portrait of Northumberland* (Robert Hale, 1965), led me to the 'land of the free'. American history had never greatly interested me and the American system of government was, and still is, a mystery. As a child I had heard about the 'Boston Tea Party' and the name Christopher Columbus, quite in the wrong order. This did not worry me then as, for some inexplicable reason, I was convinced that Columbus was a character in *Treasure Island!* It was not until the Second World War, and later the assassination of John F. Kennedy, that my interest in the USA was roused. I never imagined that my literary efforts were in libraries in foreign countries, or even in the Commonwealth, until I received a letter from a Doctor and Mrs Ridley Tipton in North Carolina. These unknown correspondents were planning a visit to England, one of many I discovered later, and asked if they could come to see me as they had read *Portrait* with great interest. Before their visit I studied an atlas to discover exactly where North Carolina was, as all I knew about this State of the Union were the titles of two dance tunes, 'Dreamy Carolina Moon' and 'Carolina in the Morning'.

My knowledge of the USA was to be considerably enlarged when I met Sam and Isabel Tipton. Isabel persuaded me to make a visit to them in North Carolina and promised that she would arrange some speaking engagements for me. I felt that this was too good an opportunity to miss and in spite of my horror of air travel (well justified in this case) I set forth on Thursday the sixth day of October in the year of Our Lord nineteen hundred and seventy-seven. Alexander Collingwood Douglas-Home Ridley, the most famous cat in the world, was left in the care of my friend Lilian, to whom this book is dedicated. Looking after Alec Ridley deserves public recognition!

I was seen off at Newcastle Central Station by several friends with all the ceremony usually only accorded to Royalty or an Ambassadress for Britain. As is customary with me, whenever I have V.I.P. treatment, I am brought down to earth with a bang or, in this case, grounded. When I reached Gatwick a strike was well under way and we were five hours late in taking off. As usual the bars were closed, though I did manage to buy a bottle of sherry which only added to my troubles, as I was to discover by the time I reached Southport, North Carolina. The usual day turning into night and vice versa has never been comprehensible to my unscientific mind and by the time we touched down at John F. Kennedy Airport I was almost certifiable. The last plane for Washington had gone so my first night was spent in a down-town hotel in New York. Having been warned by my nearest and dearest to barricade myself into my room as murders are two-a-penny in New York, I spent the night in a state of siege until I was rescued by Isabel Tipton, who had taken a shuttle service flight from Washington.

When at last we arrived at Washington, by the shuttle service, I was more or less incapable of standing and had not the resourceful Sam chartered a wheelchair to transport me to their car, I would have spent my visit in Washington Airport. The drive to Long Beach, Southport, seemed endless. It took all of nine hours as, though Americans love enormous 'automobiles' and are always in a mad rush, there is a strict speed limit on the highways and heavy fines are imposed for speeding. When we eventually arrived at the Tiptons' very comfortable but isolated home, set in what appeared to me, in my muddled condition, a huge forest, I was still clasping that celebrated bottle of sherry, only to discover that my hosts were teetotallers and non-smokers! My friends may well ask why I hadn't taken to the bottle to help me through my ordeal: the reason was I don't like sherry, it was *not* self-control.

I must have amazing powers of resilience as I was soon fighting fit and Isabel was a born organiser. My first talk was 'local', in the American sense of distance, to a History Society and my subject 'The Four Queens', which I have given countless times in the UK. Bloody Mary, Elizabeth I, Anne and Victoria are my Queens and I feel by now that I have actually met them! The Americans are avid for details about royalty, in fact they envy us and have a slight chip on the shoulder as Presidents can never inspire the same mixture of awe and admiration. As audiences I found the Americans very different from the British, or even the Canadians. They are so interested in personal details that at times I felt like something in Madame Tussauds! At a school in the backwoods where the majority of pupils were coloured, they crowded round me asking shyly if they could touch me as they had never met an English woman before. I found it extremely embarrassing. I asked the headmistress what prospects most of these children had and she said none, they would spend their lives in the neighbourhood eking out an existence with any menial work they could find, which rather refutes the slogan 'the land of opportunity'. Unemployment was rapidly increasing and strikes were a way of life. Leaflets from my publishers enclosing order forms for my books never turned up until I was in England again as there was a postal strike! The grumblers in this country should go to America and get out and about and not confine themselves to the lights of Broadway.

I have no intention of dwelling on the subject of my speaking engagements further, it would be repetitive. It is enough to say that they took place in Wilmington and Sandhills, the latter a Community College in which they had incongruously combined the names of Campbell and Macdonald. The Wilmington Club was more appropriately named The Cape Fear Historical Society as the town is on the Cape Fear River. Wilmington is a charming place, many of the old Colonial

103

F

houses have been revitalised and a great deal of slum clearance has been accomplished. In Wilmington I was interviewed on Carolina television in a programme called 'The Jim Burns Show'. Jim Burns, as his name denotes, was of Scottish extraction and an extremely pleasant man. I was sure that two tricky questions would be asked, which they were. One was, 'Did I think Britain was finished?' Like a family we all have arguments and different opinions but an outsider should beware; I quoted Wellington saying all those years ago that Britain was finished and that for once the Iron Duke was proved to be wrong. Then came, 'What did we think of our Royal Family?' As a dedicated Royalist I said that we loved and were proud of them. When it came to 'What did I think of America?' I used diplomacy and said that a visitor had no right to criticise! Some Americans at the present time should learn that lesson and refrain from interfering in our internal affairs. Readers will be surprised to learn that I did not receive a fee — for an Englishwoman to appear on what we would describe as a regional station was regarded as an honour!

After I had done my duty and showed the flag our sightseeing began. I found it fascinating but confusing to listen to the tales of the War of Independence and the Civil War, at times getting the two confused and dropping bricks by quoting 'Marching through Georgia' and my favourite 'Battle Hymn of the Republic'! My hosts were Southerners and I was offending them by repeating Northerners' songs! There is still a strong feeling between North and South though I never discovered the dividing line. Even in Carolina, in Moore County, the Jacobites haunted me. Flora Macdonald, after she and her husband emigrated to America, lived near Moore's Creek and Flora's son was wounded at the battle of that name fighting for a Hanoverian King!

There is a wonderful museum at Moore's Creek in the beautiful National Military Park, though I thought it tactless of my hosts to draw my attention to pictures of the British in defeat. It was, I am sure, a blessing that we lost the American colonies. America is a continent, not a country. Every State has different laws and customs, religious sects are countless, the colour problem is a festering sore: we could never have united the fifty states and made them governable. We owe George III a debt of gratitude. In some ways the American people are immature and many have an isolationist outlook. As I found in Canada, the New World is anything but classless and the Americans are dreadful snobs. Name-dropping is almost a social obligation and anyone who has had a relative presented at the British Court has reached the height of upmanship.

I cannot remember the exact order in which we did our sightseeing before we reached Washington, yet there were many adventures and much to see on the long trek. The town of Raleigh appealed to me greatly, where there is a magnificent bronze figure of the great West Countryman set in beautiful gardens. I sat close to Sir Walter and smoked my 'pipe', a gesture which I like to think he would have appreciated. I can never forgive James I and VI for bringing about the death of this very great sailor. We spent some time in the City of Durham! Durham, like its English counterpart, is a university city. The name of the university is Duke after the founder who also built a magnificent chapel or church as I would call it.

In contrast to universities and chapels we spent some nights with an extraordinary lady who was a friend of the Tiptons and while staying in her decaying but once obviously magnificent home I had a most unusual experience. I was driven through a forest in a covered wagon drawn by a mule named Kate! The driver was a very large young man wearing a ten gallon hat who had no control over Kate. We went Kate's way and as I have been told a kick from a mule is quite something I took the line of least resistance. Much to my astonishment we came back to the house, which I am purposely not naming, to be greeted by my hostess with the throw-away lines that she was glad the driver was all right (it didn't matter about me) as he often had fits! My guardian angel must have been busy that day. I brought home a wooden figure of a mule which is beside me while I write.

This hostess was anything but teetotal. She was armed with a bottle of rye all day from which she revived herself frequently. Yet she was a most likeable and intelligent woman even if her house was more than peculiar as far as domestic arrangements

105

were concerned. There were two bathrooms attached to my bedroom but no water! The bed linen was exquisite, the food (solid) conspicuous by its absence! The once well-kept gardens were a wilderness and the staff non-existent. I imagine Ellen's father had been a tobacco king as the estate was on the borders of Virginia. I certainly was meeting a cross section of American society.

The plumbing system at the House of the Mule was primitive in contrast to the comfort and cleanliness of the motels which I cannot praise too highly. The food in their hostelries was varied and delicious, I loved the clam soup and by British standards prices were very reasonable. The only poor meal we had was in the exclusive Smithsonian Institute in Washington. On the long drive to the capital city the roads were tree lined, thus hiding houses and villages, and the impression given was that of a sparsely populated country. It was only when passing through towns that this impression was dispelled. I talked to a policeman in a country town comparable with Hexham or Chichester in size. I remarked to the officer, who was the antithesis of the cops and robber type shown on films, that he had his gun at the ready. 'Ma'am,' he replied, 'If I hadn't my gun loaded I'd be dead within an hour.', which illustrates the appalling violence and criminal activities with which American police are faced. Four years later, as I repeat this statement, the British police are facing similar problems; problems never anticipated in Britain.

My final stay in America was in Virginia about ten miles from the centre of Washington. The weather was glorious and my accommodation most comfortable; the house was situated in rural surroundings. I had chosen the time of year well as I did in Canada, the Fall again wore all its colourful glory for me. I had read and heard so much about the American capital that many buildings and monuments seemed almost familiar. There were many new experiences for me, some emphasising the essential difference of outlook between these two English-speaking nations. Language we may have in common but characteristics are a world apart. I was shattered by the insensitivity of people who felt no shame whatsoever that one of their Presidents had been at the centre of a colossal scandal and misuse of power for personal gain. I thought I must be dreaming when I was told that we were to dine at Watergate, now the most fashionable restaurant in town! I have a packet of book matches to prove to the incredulous that this was so. Pictures of past Presidents are flashed on a screen in the main railway station, including the notorious Richard Nixon!

That was bad enough but more shattering to me was the sight-seeing tour to Arlington Cemetery. Special buses take the tourists to an information centre where more buses are waiting to take passengers to John F. Kennedy's most tasteless grave, or should one describe it as a memorial, a shrine or merely a tourist attraction. A flame burns constantly and 'drop-outs' do a roaring trade in luridly coloured paper flowers which people (not this writer) placed on the 'shrine'. My British sense of decency and respect was outraged. The cemetery covers acres of land and the headstones are like a growth of giant mushrooms. In my ignorance I could not understand from which wars the heroes' bodies had been brought home, until I was told that anyone who had served or, in the American term, been 'drafted', even if he had never been out of his own country and returned to civilian life after hostilities, had the right (honour?) to a grave in this far from peaceful 'garden' of American soil. I was learning.

Far away from J.F.K. and the serried rows of the 'fallen' was a plain white cross beside which lay a simple bunch of daffodils (in the Fall?). This was the grave of Bobby Kennedy, Attorney-Gerneral, the brother of the President, and as the world knows another victim of assassination. Why he was alone I never discovered. To me Bobby Kennedy's resting place has a poignancy utterly lacking in that of his brother's. It was with a feeling of relief that I left Arlington. In contrast to the vulgarity of the Kennedy memorial I found that of Abraham Lincoln, another victim of the assassin's bullet, one of the most magnificent memorials I have ever seen. It is a worthy tribute to a great American: the words of Lincoln's Gettysburg speech are comparable only to those of Winston Churchill — I can give no greater praise.

I left my American hosts one evening to visit an Englishman who was born at Haltwhistle in my native Northumberland. At that time William Clark was Vice-President of the World Bank. I felt that I was living in reflected glory. William's house was close to the British Embassy on the edge of a delightful park. A giant statue of Sir Winston Churchill gave the impression that he was delivering one of his famous speeches under a Union Jack which was fluttering in the mild evening breeze. A surge of pride in my country swept over me.

In contrast to the dignity of the ambassadorial surroundings was our visit to the White House. Visitors were rushed through at such break-neck speed and security was so obvious that I have no clear recollection of what I saw. I only know I was in the Lincoln Room because the fact was bellowed at the crowd from a loudspeaker. What furniture I could see behind the mass of cosmopolitan, hot and bemused-looking humanity was French. Thank God Buckingham Palace and Number 10 are not open to the public. The Capitol on its hill dominates this part of the city, while the Washington Memorial, resembling a giant Cleopatra's needle, towers above all. I hate heights and did not make the perilous ascent to the top, which I believe many people do. I was intrigued when we ate our most unappetising lunch in the Smithsonian Institution that this vast building which houses a collection of scientific and cultural knowledge was founded by the gift of £100,000 by Hugh Smithson Percy, the illegitimate son of the first Duke of Northumberland. It was established by an act of Congress in 1846.

Washington has an air of prosperity and wealth yet there is a very seamy side hidden away from the tourist beat. On our drives to and from my hosts in Virginia we passed through districts that can only be described as ghettos. Those in England who at this time are making such an outcry about what are termed inner city problems should see the 'outer' cities of America. I am delighted that the chance to visit even a small part of the USA came my way. I was impressed by Washington but it had not the feeling of enchantment I experienced in Victoria, British Columbia. My kind hostess and guide Isabel Tipton died last year and Sam is very ill. I hope that when he recovers and my book is published he will realise how much I appreciated his kindness and that of Isabel.

When I left for home I was assured nothing could happen as it had done on my outward flight. How wrong my well-wishers were! The plane was crowded and when we touched down at Prestwick, having passed over my beloved Hebrides in the dawn, I thought of getting off and making the rest of the journey by train. The problem was my luggage, which was labelled Gatwick, so I flew on to my fate. The gremlins had been laying their evil plans! When we landed the porters were refusing to unload the baggage — why, naturally, was a mystery. For more than four hours a mass of raging passengers were stranded. Tempers became frayed and to my horror fighting broke out and the police were brought in. I had never witnessed such scenes and I was petrified. To my astonishment a man came from nowhere, or so it seemed, called me Nancy and said he was keeping an eye on me. My protector (the wrong word!) was a doctor from Hexham who was born in the same village as I and at whose twenty-first birthday party I had been a guest almost a lifetime ago. Eventually the porters decided they had created enough trouble for the long-suffering British public and started to unload. Round and round went the turntable until nothing was left. My luggage had disappeared. This was the last straw. An airport official conjured up a large gin and tonic for me and, feeling a little better, I made for King's Cross, my handbag and passport my only possessions. I fell into the arms of my friends when the train pulled in to Number Nine Platform at Newcastle. I had never realised that Number Nine is the most wonderful platform in the world.

When I came into my own house Alec went completely mad with joy, his travelled old Mum had come home. Much telephoning had to be done in efforts to trace my missing luggage and, as I do not possess a large wardrobe, I spent more than a week in 'uniform'. Alec alerted me one morning that a strange car was in the compound (my name for the yard behind our terrace of houses). A Securicor van was pulling up at my door — my luggage had followed me home. One bag had been to Brazil, while the less adventurous of the two had called only at Northampton. It is now four years since I have been airborne and I have vowed that never again will I tempt providence. Resolutions are often broken — I vowed that I would never write another book!

CHAPTER THIRTEEN
HEROES IN MY LIFETIME

With malice towards none; with charity for all;
with firmness in the right, as God gives us to see the right.

Abraham Lincoln, 1863

THESE WORDS of a great American seem to be the most appropriate in our common language to epitomise the qualities of the four people whom I regard as heroes in my lifetime: Her Majesty Queen Elizabeth the Queen Mother, a Scot; Lord Home of The Hirsel, also a Scot; P.C. Trevor Lock of the Iranian Embassy siege, an Englishman; and the greatest wartime leader in our history, an Englishman whose mother was an American. With the exception of Sir Winston my heroes are all living today and I hope for many years to come. My mother had a philosophy, which I feel should be practised more generally, and that was to tell people when they are alive that we admire and love them and resist the fashion to eulogise them in fulsome obituaries. The British find it extremely difficult, in fact embarrassing, to display emotion, it is very much easier to express in written words one's admiration. Of the four people I admire so greatly I have met only one. I have contempt for name-droppers and those who on a brief acquaintance refer to the great and famous as their friends. I regard such behaviour as the height of presumption and bad taste.

I have never had the privilege of a presentation to a member of the Royal Family and I admit that on some occasions when Her Majesty the Queen Mother has been quite close to my home I have felt disappointed and hurt that I have not been deemed worthy of the honour. I have been fortunate enough to see Her Majesty at close quarters on several occasions and such is her radiance and charm that I have had a lump in my throat just to look at her. The first time I saw her was in 1938 when as a

111

young Queen she accompanied her husband King George VI to Newcastle upon Tyne when His Majesty launched the battleship named after his father, the *King George V*. I remember that Queen Elizabeth was dressed in a deep shade of purple and wearing, as was universal in those far-off days, a silver fox fur. The King was in naval uniform. The *K.G.V.* as the ship was known to all Tynesiders survived the Second World War and was the first 'ship of the line' to which our present Queen paid a visit after hostilities ceased. The *K.G.V.* was one of the last ships of her type to be built and long ago was broken up at Rosyth.

I was in the vast crowd on Coronation Day who saw The Queen Mother driving in the procession accompanied by Her Royal Highness Princess Margaret. The closest and best view I had was due to a kindly policeman who arranged for me to have a vantage point at the Northumberland Plate of 1963. This time Her Majesty wore the most exquisite green outfit, a colour which someone described as translucent. Then in her early sixties she was lovelier than ever and the men were going down like skittles. Once when staying on Deeside I was fortunate enough to see The Queen Mother and Princess Margaret driving to Crathie Church for morning service. Princess Margaret was young and unmarried. She was so ethereal-looking that an onlooker compared her with a porcelain figure.

So many books and articles have been written about this best-loved member of the Royal Family that I have been under the impression that everyone was familar with her background. This curiously is not always the case. I was asked the other day if she had a title before she married the then Duke of York! To me it seems superfluous to explain that she was Lady Elizabeth Angela Marguerite Bowes-Lyon, the youngest daughter of the 14th Earl of Strathmore and Kinghorne, and was born on the 4th of August 1900 in London. In 1923 she married the Duke of York who, after the abdication of King Edward VIII, became our sixth King George, ascending to the throne in 1937. The most shattering experience of ignorance regarding 'The Queen Mum', as she is affectionately known, was when a Canadian history graduate of Vancouver University visited me. I was telling this 'educated' young lady how much we all love The Queen Mum. Looking puzzled, my visitor said, 'Who is The Queen Mum?' I was so shaken it took me some time to stammer out, 'Well, the Queen's mother, of course.' Worse was to come from the 'historian'; 'I never knew the Queen had a mother, and if she had I thought she would be Queen Victoria!' Our discussion on British royalty ended somewhat abruptly.

In all the books and articles written about The Queen Mother I can find no reference to the Bowes-Lyon connections in my own county of Northumberland. Ridley Hall in South Tynedale was the property of the Hon. Francis Bowes-Lyon for many years. To use an expression 'up with which' Sir Winston would 'not have put', I have explored every avenue but cannot trace any written records of the then Lady Elizabeth Bowes-Lyon ever having stayed at Ridley Hall. The widow of Sir James Bowes-Lyon, who lives at the nearby Beltingham House, has told me that Her Majesty often talks about Northumberland, so one might reasonably assume that she visited Ridley Hall before her marriage to the Duke of York.

I have discovered some very interesting information from my friend Mrs Clark of Featherstone Castle which she has kindly given me permission to repeat. During the last war the King and Queen were on a secret visit to Tyneside, travelling in the royal train. For safety and security the train was halted for the night at Featherstone Park railway station on the now defunct Haltwhistle to Alston line. Featherstone Castle was then a boys' school and their Majesties, when out for an evening walk, made an unexpected visit to the Castle. Excited boys were brought from their dormitories in their dressing gowns to the windows of the ground floor and their royal guests spoke to some of them. This little-known incident was featured in an article by Michael Wilcox in the Hexham Courant in 1980 to mark the anniversary of the Queen Mother's 80th birthday. I have been told, but cannot vouch for the veracity of the story, that an old man who lived in the Park village was standing at the door when the royal couple approached and that the Queen recognised him as a man who had once worked at Glamis.

One of this royal lady's most endearing qualities is her ability to talk to ordinary people without any air of patronage. This I attribute to her upbringing on great estates where tenants and employees are treated as friends. This applies especially in Scotland where the clan spirit is still strong. I have twice been the guest of the present Earl and Countess of Strathmore at Glamis and once at Holwick in Teesdale, where the Bowes-Lyon family still owns land. An anecdote has just come into my mind which exemplifies what I have said about Her Majesty's gift of doing and saying the right thing at every function she attends. When the Royal Show came to Newcastle upon Tyne at the end of its touring life, the Queen Mother was the guest of honour. As she was being shown round she noticed a group of canteen workers who were being kept at a distance. Imagine their pleasure when she walked over to them and asked one of them where she came from. 'Scotland,' was the reply. 'So do I,' said Her Majesty. It is this genuine interest and sincerity which is part of The Queen Mum's charm.

I do not think it is sufficiently realised what tremendous help and support she gave to her husband who broke down and cried when he had to take up the burden of kingship abrogated by his brother. Hampered as the new King was by a speech defect it was his Queen who was always with him when he broadcast or spoke in public. In a letter he wrote to our present Queen he spoke of 'Mummy' as the most wonderful person in the world. In this humble subject's opinion she is the woman of the century. Her love of racing is well-known and it was a grief shared by the nation when Devon Loch collapsed (the reason will never be known) when to all intents and purposes he had won the National. The owner's remark is typical. When Dick Francis, the jockey, was received in the royal box there were no recriminations, resignedly the owner said 'That's racing.'

It seems appropriate that I should end this short appreciation of the most greatly loved royal consort on her birthday, the fourth of August 1981, when Her Majesty is eighty-one years young. The nation felt a surge of love and relief last week when Her Majesty was sufficiently recovered from her recent illness to attend the wedding of her favourite grandchild His Royal

Highness the Prince of Wales to Lady Diana Spencer. It brought tears to the eyes of millions who watched the fairy-tale ceremony on television as the crowds in the Mall called repeatedly for The Queen Mum to come out onto the balcony, where she herself made her appearance as a bride fifty-eight years ago. The appreciation which to me conveyed so much in a minimum of words was, 'Thank Your Majesty for just being The Queen Mum.'

A peacetime hero of recent times who was decorated by his Sovereign is the latest hero I have added to my list. Were I, which is most unlikely, to be asked again to talk about my heroes on television, which I did in January 1981, P.C. Trevor Lock would be included. To write of this Metropolitan police constable gives me the opportunity to express in words my admiration and support for the entire British police force. Without the whole-hearted support of the public and respect for law and order Britain could become a nation where anarchy prevails. Police at times do make mistakes and errors of judgement. This is inevitable in any class of society. There are good and bad in every walk of life; a 'bent' policeman is no more extraordinary than, for example, a bank manager who misappropriates a customer's money, or a solicitor who betrays the trust in which his client holds him. Members of the medical profession have at times broken the ethics governing their practice. Members of Parliament have fallen foul of the law, while 'fiddling' the Inland Revenue has become almost acceptable. Many prominent figures have been 'guests of Her Majesty' and one could go on endlessly quoting examples of malpractice.

My contacts with both Metropolitan and Provincial Forces have always, so far, been on the right side of the law, so I may be forgiven if I am somewhat prejudiced in my views. I am the proud possessor of Sir Robert Mark's autobiography *In the Office of Constable* (Collins, 1978), signed for me by this outstanding ex-Commissioner of the Metropolitan Police. Sir Robert held a signing session in Newcastle, followed by a luncheon in the Civic Centre when he gave a short speech. He is

115

the only writer I have met who disclosed in public the small percentage the writer receives from the selling price of a book. I felt that Sir Robert had done me a personal service, as I cannot convince people that I am not a wealthy woman. My bank manager can vouch for this fact! Now it is Sir David McNee who holds the 'office of constable'.

At the present time when the police of this country and Northern Ireland are facing outbreaks of violence on a scale out of keeping with the British way of life, the 'do-gooders' have a field day if a policeman fails in his duty. The new sport of police bashing is a favourite pastime of the self-styled intelligentsia. Little sympathy is shown towards the victims of assault and 'mugging' — the police are the whipping boys. The British Police Force is the best in the world and P.C. Lock is a shining example of all that is best in the force. Details of this brave man were given to me by Scotland Yard; my approach to the 'Yard' was made at the suggestion of the Northumbria Police. To ring the best-known telephone number in the country I admit excited me greatly and I was given clearance to write an appreciation which gratified me enormously.

Trevor Lock was born on 14th April 1939 at Dagenham, Essex. He chose as his career to enter the force founded by Sir Robert Peel in 1829. The reason why policemen are known as bobbies is to commemorate the christian name of this great Lancastrian who was Prime Minister in the second administration of Queen Victoria's reign. After the twelve weeks' training, which to me appears to be much too short, Trevor Lock became a bobbie on the beat at Barking. He was a member of the Metropolitan Police which is 25,000 strong. My hero from Essex transferred from the 'bobbie on the beat' section to a specialised branch, the Diplomatic Protection Group, and it was while on duty at the Iranian Embassy in London that, by his coolness and adherence to the strict rules of his calling, he became a national figure.

It was in April 1980 while guarding the Embassy that he was taken at gunpoint by terrorists and held hostage for six days with members of the Embassy staff. It was not until his release that his level-headed behaviour became known to the public.

The terrorists were unaware that he was armed and he managed to conceal the fact throughout the siege. He was escorted even to the 'loo' by members of the gang, so he refused to take any liquid he was offered as the gun was hidden in his trousers! After six days in which he had little or no sleep the S.A.S. stormed the Embassy and the terrorists became trigger-happy. While struggling with one of his captors, though his gun lay only inches away, P.C. Lock did not use it. He said afterwards that the urge to use it was strong but, remembering his training and the strict control on the use of firearms which is the police code, he resisted the temptation.

When I saw the S.A.S. in action on television I thought at first it was a cloak-and-dagger film, then I realised it was reality and the hostages were free. Two of the terrorists died during the operation which, of course, roused the sympathy of the 'do-gooders'. Surely when under fire from would-be murderers self protection comes first, or should the murderers be asked to sit down and have a cosy chat before killing their victims? These outbursts have no sense of proportion. I wonder what the do-gooders would have done under such circumstances? The unsung heroes of this siege were the anonymous members of the S.A.S.

It is a sad indictment of our so-called civilised society that after the event P.C. Lock, his wife and six children were harassed and abused by hooligans and thugs, who daubed their home with the word 'pig', which is their obscene name for the police. Dagenham should have given the man in blue a hero's welcome instead of driving him from his home. That courage and integrity have their reward was testified when in the Birthday Honours List P.C. Lock was awarded the George Medal. This is the highest honour for outstanding bravery in peacetime. The news of his decoration was given to him on his 42nd birthday. I watched and listened to Trevor Lock on 'the box' when he left the Investiture at Buckingham Palace and was impressed by his manner and modesty. He remarked that in a year's time he will be forgotten and people will say if his name is mentioned 'Trevor who?' In this I disagree with him, he is a lasting source of pride to responsible members of the public and

117

his deed added more lustre to 'the thin blue line'.

With men like Trevor Lock, and there are many who never hit the headlines, Britain can once more be 'Great' and Her Majesty feel proud of the men who take the oath of allegiance. Perhaps the ghost of Sir Robert Peel was with another Sovereign Lady on the 15th July 1981, the day of the Investiture. He would have taken great pride in his namesake's devotion to duty. On the 29th of July 1981, the Royal Wedding day, the British police showed the world that they have no equals, and by their good-humoured control over the vast crowds in London, their efficient and discreet methods of security, must have made their critics and denigrators feel small. That is, if people of that type have the sensitivity to realise that they are a tiny and discredited minority. Constable Trevor Lock must have been a proud man on that great day to be one of the thousands of bobbies who protect the lives and liberties of Her Majesty's subjects.

When I was a guest in the television programme *Heroes* I chose Lord Home of the Hirsel as one of my favourite politicians. Of the four people I am writing about in this chapter Lord Home is the only one I have met and talked with. This, for me, momentous meeting took place in Lord Home's own country, the Border town of Coldstream, to be followed later by an official introduction in my own county of Northumberland at the Collingwood Arms in Cornhill-on-Tweed. Lord Home was then Prime Minister and the characteristics which struck me so forcibly were his modesty, sincerity and lack of pomposity. I have beside me as I write a copy of his autobiography *The Way the Wind Blows* (Collins, 1970) and I am quoting part of an appreciation of Lord Home by Robert Blake of the Oxford Mail, which appears on the jacket to the book ' . . . the nicest, least arrogant, most honourable and least lucky of all our modern Prime Ministers'. His integrity is like a light in a political world which does not embody, or only on rare occasions, these essential qualities. He is the last of the outstanding and natural leaders of my generation.

Born a countryman, with a deep love of the Border land, he

118

reminds me in some ways of a Northumbrian who also served his Sovereign with loyalty and integrity, Viscount Grey of Fallodon. Those who study family relationships, which are abundant in Northumberland and the Borders, will know that there are blood connections between the Scottish family of Home and the English one of Grey. Both men held the position of Secretary of State for Foreign Affairs, though in different parties and times, Lord Home as a Tory and Lord Grey as a Liberal. Both men loved nature and wildlife, especially birds, yet in each case their political lives kept them away from their home backgrounds for long intervals. Lord Home overcame a long and painful illness which incapacitated him for some considerable time, while Lord Grey struggled for years against failing eyesight.

When Lord Home was chosen to lead the Conservative Party after the resignation of Harold Macmillan, he renounced his peerage as 14th Earl of Home to enable him to sit in the Commons. For reasons known only to himself, Sir Harold Wilson, as he now is, thought it clever to make sarcastic remarks about 'the 14th Earl' which drove the naturally gentle Sir Alec Douglas-Home, as he now is known, to retort, 'You are the 14th Mr Wilson!' Readers can correctly assume that the former Mr Wilson is not one of my favourite men. The reason why peers may not enter the Commons goes back in time to the arrest of the five members in the days of the despotic Charles I. There is an anecdote about this rule in William Douglas-Home's book *Mr Home Pronounced Hume*, (Collins, 1979) which illustrates this ban as practised in modern times. When Lord Home, then Lord Dunglass, was told of his father's death he was already a member of Parliament. He had left his hat and coat in the House and he was not allowed to collect them himself, a policeman had to fetch them for him.

I am not equipped nor, if I were, would I attempt to assess Lord Home's political career. History will pronounce its verdict with, of course, the benefit of hindsight. On his retirement from the political scene Sir Alec (and that is how I always think of him) was created a life peer in 1974, taking the title of Lord Home of the Hirsel. Born in 1903 he entered

119

politics in 1931 when he won the marginal seat of South Lanark. In 1951 he was made a Privy Councillor and became Foreign Secretary under Sir Harold Macmillan and Prime Minister from 1963-1964. He is also a member of Scotland's most ancient Order of Chivalry, the Knights of the Thistle. Sir Alec attributes his appearances on television as one of the reasons for his defeat in the 1964 general election. He admits that he was never at ease and, to use the present-day jargon, he did not have the image which a 'goggle-box' audience expects. I feel this is an indictment of present day life that sense of values have become so blurred. Some of the 'glamour boy' politicians are not exactly outstanding members of the Mother of Parliaments!

I share one of my hero's interests, racing, and without presumption a shared interest makes one feel closer and more able to understand people, even if they are great and famous. I have beside me a letter from Lord Home which demonstrates his lack of pomposity and his delicious sense of humour. When I chose him as a hero I wrote to tell Lord Home so and mentioned that my eighteen-year-old cat Alec, who is named after the famous Borderer, was also appearing on this programme. His Lordship's comment was: 'How nice of you to alert me to Alec's appearance on T.V. I shall feel reflected glory!' That letter is now in my Alec's snob book. I play One Upmanship by prominently displaying my autographed copy of *Border Reflections* (Collins, 1979).

Two other Prime Ministers rank high in my admiration, respect and affection: Disraeli (not in my lifetime!) and Sir Winston Churchill, who also appeared in my list of heroes on the television programme. People may say that there is nothing more to write about the great war leader. Countless biographies have been written; his speeches have been collected and published, yet very few ordinary people who lived through the war years have expressed their feelings in print. Through the darkest days of 1939-1945 I never once contemplated defeat for the Allies. Churchill was there to ensure victory, to give us heart with speeches comparable only with those of Abraham Lincoln.

Winston Churchill 'walked with kings, nor lost the common touch' and the sense of shame felt by myself and those round me when the man who had saved not only Britain but the world was rejected by the electorate still hurts. In contrast to the dark days I vividly remember the cheers that greeted Sir Winston on Coronation Day and how proud I was to be among that vast rain-drenched crowd in Hyde Park when Duchess Sarah's descendant rode in the carriage procession (wearing the wrong hat with his Trinity House uniform). Security was not so stringent as now and a friend of mine actually got close to the carriage and touched the great man.

Although entirely different characters, Sir Winston and Lord Home share the ability to reach the hearts of people by simple, kindly gestures. After the tragedy of the 1945 election I wrote to Mr Churchill (he had not then been knighted nor received the Order of the Garter) and he replied to my letter in his own handwriting. A lesser man would have sent a photostat or a secretary would have sent a stereotyped message. That letter is framed and has a place of honour in the room where I am writing. My dear mother, who was unable to grasp that anyone 'nice' could be anything but a Tory, would draw visitors' attention to 'Winston's letter', whatever their politics.

Some years ago I made a pilgrimage to Blenheim to see the room where Winston Spencer Churchill was born and made my way to the quiet little churchyard at Bladen to pay homage at the simple grave where the old warrior rests. Being something of a sentimentalist I wondered last week if his ghost was at the royal wedding, exulting that a daughter of the Spencer family was marrying the heir to the throne. How he would have revelled in the pomp and pageantry!

I deplore and despise the present cult of those who do their utmost to prove that our idols had feet of clay. It is some form of jealousy exhibited by those who do not possess the talents of those they denigrate and who could never achieve the heights to which the heroes have risen. The backstairs gossip columns of the gutter press are the products of sick minds. There is a saying that the hour produces the man: at times this seems a vague hope yet, in the years to come when Britain is great again, future generations may be blessed with another 'Queen Mum' almost as gracious and 'giving' but never equalling the one who said, 'I come from Scotland, too.': another Trevor Lock may wear the blue uniform and uphold the traditions of the British police: and from the political wilderness may emerge statesmen, not career men, of the calibre of Churchill and Home who devoted their lives to their country without fear or favour. All four of whom I have written could have been the inspiration for the hymn sung at the wedding of the century:

> *I vow to thee my Country, all earthly things above,*
> *Entire and whole and perfect, the service of my love;*
> *The love that asks no questions, the love that stands the*
> *test,*
> *That lays upon the altar the dearest and the best;*
> *The love that never falters, the love that pays the price,*
> *The love that makes undaunted the final sacrifice.*
> Sir Cecil Spring-Rice,
1856-1918

CHAPTER FOURTEEN

YE HIGHLANDS, YE LOWLANDS

Should auld acquaintance be forgot,
And never brought to mind?
Should auld acquaintance be forgot,
And auld lang syne?

Robert Burns

BORN AS I was in a Border county which through the centuries until the Union of the Crowns was a buffer state between two countries, I regard myself as neither English nor Scottish but Northumbrian, with at times divided loyalties. It therefore seems appropriate to end this book with a chapter entirely devoted to Scotland, the country I know and love second only to my own Northumberland.

The many Scots who are my friends are the antithesis of the false image held by so many of the English. The blame for this I attribute to many of the Scots themselves, who for commercial reasons have built up an exaggerated picture.

If by writing this chapter I can in some measure dispel the 'image' that every Scotsman wears the kilt; his entire diet is composed of haggis and porridge, and whisky is the equivalent of early morning tea, then I have achieved my object.

I have some sympathy with those who believe the many misconceptions. Scottish history is a mass of confusion; the early Scots came from Ireland, the Angles populated the Lowlands, and then some Scots returned to Ulster! The Scottish Kings were monarchs of the Scots, not of Scotland, there were invariably many claimants to the throne, and to the Scottish nobles loyalty was often more in favour of themselves than of the throne, this division of loyalties was the curse of Scotland. Ironically it was a Scottish King, the very unattractive James VI, who succeeded to the England throne.

Before 1603 the Scots were not only constantly at war with England but at war amongst themselves.

If it were possible the religious bigotry was deeper than that of England. John Knox, who is not one of my favourite men, is a glaring example of intolerance. To regard all Scots as members of the Presbyterian Church of Scotland is another myth. Certainly it is the established Church, but numerically there are more Roman Catholics, Episcopalians and smaller sects which outnumber the Establishment. That this appalling bigotry has crumbled into dust was exemplified at the marriage of H.R.H. The Prince of Wales and Lady Diana Spencer, when not only the Archbishop of Canterbury officiated, but the Moderator of the General Assembly of the Church of Scotland and the Roman Catholic Archbishop of Westminster took part in the service.

To many Scots it is regarded as an insult to be mistaken for Glaswegians yet this great mass of the industrial area of Clydeside, now renamed Strathclyde though it is only a part of the original Strathclyde, does contain half the country's population. A minority may be drunken and unruly but they do not represent the many law-abiding and distinguished Glaswegians and like all minorities, they hit the headlines. As it is easy to generalise those who do not know Scotland imagine that this minority is representative of the country as a whole. This is entirely untrue. Nothing could be more different from the Celtic-Rangers annual soccer match, which in fact is Irish Roman Catholicism versus Protestant Scot, than the Rugby Union which flourishes on the Borders, culminating in the Calcutta Cup played at Murrayfield. (When I last was a spectator at The Calcutta Cup match I cheered for England in the first half and Scotland in the second. How much further can one carry neutrality?) Shinty is played in the Highlands where few Rugby or Soccer teams exist. To puzzle the reader once more, Berwick Association Football Club plays in the Scottish League, and for those who are ignorant of the fact, the town of Berwick is in England.

Glasgow has a world famous choir, the Glasgow Orpheus Choir, while the Art Gallery houses a superb collection, yet I venture to guess that to many people the reputation of the Gorbals is more familiar! The most famous of the many Scottish comedians, Sir Harry Lauder, 'belonged to Glasgow' although born in Portobello, near Edinburgh. My favourite Scottish comedian of modern times is Stanley Baxter, his impersonations of the ladies of Kelvinside (very refained) used to convulse me with laughter when he appeared in *The Five Past Eight Show* with Jimmy Logan. To have the ability to make others happy and take them away even for a short time from this chaotic and restless world in which we live is an admirable gift.

I have been fortunate from an early age to travel throughout the Kingdom of Scots, usually with a purpose to follow in the footsteps of those historical figures who have captured my imagination, and to see for myself the places where they played out their parts in the drama which is history. I must have travelled not hundreds but thousands of miles to gather material for my talks and literary efforts. I refuse to use the word research; it would be pretentious. I look back with pleasure and sometimes with nostalgia to those many journeys which have become part of my life.

I have sailed to the Outer and Inner Hebrides, to Orkney and Shetland, Iona and Staffa. Those who have visited the sacred Isle of Iona (recently acquired by the Scottish National Trust, when it was put on the market by the Duke of Argyll) will remember that a perilous descent has to be made by a rope ladder from MacBrayne's steamer into a far from steady rowing boat. I was fascinated by the 'blue rinsed' mommas who stayed aboard writing postcards. They didn't venture on deck! We landed on Staffa at our own risk as large notice boards proclaimed. I doubt if I could risk such a hazardous adventure now. Perhaps one day I may summon the strength to write in detail of the many expeditions I have made. I am horrified to discover that some writers never visit the places they write about with such apparent authority. In some cases their powers of imagination have resulted in their books becoming best-sellers, that is something which will never happen to me. It is very hard not to become bitter and cynical, and not to query

125

every so-called fact mentioned by some of these writers. No one is infallible and I realise only too well that I have made glaring mistakes and still do, but at least I have endured and suffered discomfort and made every effort to familiarise myself with my subjects. If I have failed it is my fault and mine alone. I cannot bear those people who apportion all blame to circumstances.

Islands have a fascination for me and I love the sea; for someone who becomes hysterical in a 'plane, the sea holds no terrors for me. My ability to eat an enormous meal while crossing the Pentland Firth, which is always rough, amazed the Captain. I was the only passenger in the saloon, the others were below waiting for a watery grave! Orkney and Shetland have no kinship with the Scottish mainland, they are, or were, entirely Norse. How much effect the exploitation of North Sea oil has had on their way of life I have no first hand knowledge; detrimental I should imagine. I have no desire to go back! I wish to remember them before they were 'discovered'. St Magnus Cathedral made a great impression on me, within its ancient walls is the memorial to the men of *Royal Oak* who lost their lives when a German submarine penetrated the defence nets and torpedoed the great ship as she lay close to the shore. The Churchill Barrier over which I crossed to St Margaret Hope was built at the orders of Sir Winston after the disaster. In 1916 Lord Kitchener went down in the *Hampshire* off the Orcadian coast. Those were the days of the great ships which lay in Scapa Flow, familiar to so many in the days of the First and Second World Wars. The huge mass of Sumburgh Head and the sight of the Fair Isle are my most vivid recollections of Shetland, and the streets of Lerwick which one climbed by holding on to a handrail with, as I remember counting, seven different churches of worship.

I have already described my Hebridean journeys when I was following Prince Charlie. On the mainland I have covered Scotland from the Carter Bar to John O'Groats, sailed the length of the Caledonian Canal, camped on the shores of Loch Lomond, and been a guest in some of the most famous and historic castles, and on many occasions joined the queues which Scotland's stately homes attract.

The most dramatic scenery is to be seen in Sutherland, where I would happily return tomorrow. Ben Loyal and Ben Hope tower like giants over the plain from which they rise in splendid isolation. The great sandy bays stretch for miles, as yet unspoilt by man. Caithness I found a sad county, there are too many memories of the Clearances, as there are in Sutherland. Glen Naver is haunted by the ghosts of those evicted from their homes to make way for the coming of the sheep. I admit to trespassing to get a close view of the Castle of Mey, the ruin rescued and restored by Her Majesty the Queen Mother. There, in that wild and isolated setting, Her Majesty can enjoy the privacy denied her in her more accessible homes. She is reputed to have said that her Caithness home 'is out of this world'. Apocryphal or not it is the perfect description.

It was on that same foray that my Scottish friend who was acting as guide and chauffeur drove me along the shores of Loch Assynt where we gazed on the ruins that still stand on the island where the Great Montrose was foully betrayed to his enemies by a Macleod. It was left to 'King' Campbell to carry out the order of execution of the greatest Scotsman of them all. Montrose who was no mean poet wrote the following lines,

He either fears his Fate too much.
Or his Deserts are small,
That puts it not unto the Touch,
To win or lose it all.

Whenever I have travelled down the Great Glen I have thought of Montrose in his hours of glory when he trapped the Campbells in their own country. It seems almost superfluous to add that 'King' Campbell was aboard a ship so that he could make his escape. The Clansmen fought, not their Chief! It is not surprising that on Drumossie Moor where the clansmen lie in the Long Graves the Campbells are buried in isolation. I realise only too well that I talk too much and air my historical opinions with no holds barred; sometimes this can lead to embarrassing encounters. Not long ago I shared a table in a local café with a middle aged man who was extremely voluble. He was a Scot and asked me if I was interested in Highland history. 'Yes,' said I,

127

'especially in Montrose and those despicable Campbells'. With blazing eyes and almost shaking with anger, the fatal words were spoken, 'Madam, I am a Campbell.' The Clans or tribes, if one cares to call them such, were broken after the '45. The tartan was banned; no Highlander could carry arms. It was not until the end of the eighteenth century that these bans were lifted. The clan system has vanished but the spirit remains and Highland pride is strong. When last I was in Angus, which is well south of the Highland Line, my host observed to another guest that I was anti-Campbell. 'Who wouldn't be,' was the laconic comment. I may add that my host's surname was highland.

Not long ago I spent a couple of nights in a restored fourteenth century tower on the South Esk. Originally the property of an Ogilvy, it was later owned by a family named Lyall, who sold it in 1974. It is a miracle that Inverquharity Castle was not in a more ruinous condition when it became the property of Mr and Mrs Alexander Grant. The tower had not been occupied since the days of the Ogilvys. Surprisingly, when one reads the history of Scotland which is a record of burning and pillage, Inverquharity escaped, only the ravages of time and vandalism took their toll. Unfortunately from my point of view there is very little history to record. Inverquharity is not as one would expect pronounced as it is written, very few Scottish names are, and I had to practise the correct pronunciation, which I cannot express in phonetic spelling. The little personal history I did discover was that an Alexander Ogilvy was out with Montrose, was wounded at Aberdeen and managed to reach the safety of his home. There Alexander was 'panned' (nursed) by James Ramsey, until he was able to rejoin Montrose. Captured by the enemy he was executed in Glasgow. The 'yett' (iron gate) outside the main door of Inverquharity dates from the middle of the fifteenth century, the licence to fortify granted by James II still survives. Never before where I have been a guest have I been told to look upwards to the roof where are Murder Holes. Through these holes missiles or boiling lead, if it was handy, were used as a greeting for unwelcome visitors. The custom fell into disuse long years ago.

A well forty feet in depth was discovered during excavations in what is now the morning room, I was much relieved to find it had a strong cover. I am not an authority on fourteenth century architecture and have no intention of posing as such. There is an excellent booklet, a joint effort by Mr and Mrs Grant, describing the remarkable restoration which they have achieved.

Several years ago I was smuggled into another castle, Kilravock in Nairnshire, by a kind friend who risked her reputation for my sake. This was a Gathering of the Rose Clan of which my friend's mother was a member. It was an unforgettable spectacle. The Chief of Clan Rose is a woman, Miss Elizabeth Rose, who came out from Kilravock preceded by her Piper and Standard Bearer. This was the Scotland of the genuine tartan, the men in Rose tartan kilts and the women in tartan skirts (a woman should never wear a kilt). The Pipes in a setting such as this gathering were superb. Bagpipes should be played outside and Northumbrian pipes indoors. The skirl of the pipes has a rousing effect; through centuries they have played Highland troops into battle. Oddly enough there are two famous pipe bands in Northumberland; The Rothbury and Morpeth Pipe Bands. In the '45 the Chief of Clan Rose sat on the fence. He must have been a master of diplomacy, or an expert 'trimmer'. I would suggest that he was all things to all men. In early April of 1746 he has the unique experience of entertaining the leaders of the opposing forces at Kilravock. Charles Edward Stuart spent a night in the castle and after his departure on the ill-fated road to Culloden William Augustus, Duke of Cumberland, was the next Royal visitor to honour (though that term is hardly applicable to the 'Butcher') Rose with his presence. Cumberland remarked to Rose that he understood his cousin had spent the previous night at Kilravock. 'That is so, Sire' replied Rose. 'Quite correct,' said Stinking Billy. Rose was one of the few to retain his lands and escape the aftermath of the '45. The castle is now a Christian Guest House; Miss Elizabeth having got religion in a big way. When my companion and I discovered that guests were not permitted to smoke or indulge in the demon drink, we beat a hasty retreat!

Perhaps the most exciting of my visits to Scottish castles was to the Bonnie House of Airlie, as Airlie Castle is so often called. Reputed to be the smallest castle in the British Isles, it is absolutely enchanting. Set upon high ground above gorges through which flow the Isla and Melgum burns thus forming a natural fortification, Airlie is the most cosy castle it has been my privilege to explore. I was invited by the Dowager Countess of Airlie, whom I had met when a guest at nearby Glamis (who says she doesn't name-drop!) and I have Lady Airlie's written permission to write my impressions. To write fully the history of this ancient and noble family would require at least two chapters, therefore I am confining myself to some of the human side of Airlie's stormy history. As we walked round the grounds Lady Airlie drew my attention to two shrubs in the shape of hearts. Her story was that one of Queen Victoria's Prime Ministers, The Earl of Rosebery, and his bride Hannah Rothschild spent part of their honeymoon at Airlie and these heart shaped shrubs were planted to commemorate the event. There is an avenue of laburnums planted on the occasion of the Golden Wedding of the late Earl and his wife, the present Dowager.

The burning of the Bonnie House which took place in 1640 is told in verse, not altogether accurate, in the Ballad of that name. Set to music, The Bonnie House was played by pipers at the marriage of Her Royal Highness Princess Alexandra and the Honourable Angus Ogilvy in 1963. Not surprisingly the burning was one of the Campbells' many crimes. The Lady Airlie of 1640 was driven from her home and forced to watch the destruction of the Ogilvy heritage. Lord Airlie was absent at the time; the Campbells always took advantage of such opportunities. The ballad would have us believe that Lady Airlie died from exposure; in reality she survived and bore another child. (Her husband did return!) The Ogilvys were 'out' in the '15 and the '45, always loyal to the House of Stuart; some lost their lands, some their lives; the fortunate managed to escape, often in a melodramatic manner. Some may laugh at me for this anecdote which follows, but to me it made all the grandeur and famous names so very human. Lying on the terrace was a tortoiseshell cat which Lady Airlie asked me to pick up and tell her if I thought she (the cat) was going to have kittens. Rabbie Burns would have said, 'The rank is but the guinea's stamp, The man's the gowd for a' that.' I cannot resist quoting the first verse of the ballad as my Farewell to Airlie.

> *It fell on a day, a bonnie summer day*
> *When the corn was brearin' fairly,*
> *There fell out a great dispute,*
> *Atween Argyle and Airlie.*

So many memories are coming to life it will be impossible to dwell on them all; so many life-long ambitions have been achieved, some in the most unexpected ways.

When I finished my chapters on Charles II, I had to omit his Scottish Coronation as I had not been to Scone and, sticking to my rule of never to write about places unless I had actually been there, I regretted this omission. I can now rectify this. Only ten days ago I walked down the Long Gallery at Scone Palace in the steps of Charles on his way to the only Presbyterian Coronation Service ever held. It was the last Coronation ceremony held in Scotland. In 1651 Charles was crowned King of Scots on the Moot Hill; part of the church still remains. The poor young man, he was only twenty, was subjected to a sermon (no doubt stressing hell-fire and damnation) which lasted for an hour and a half. No wonder that after his restoration in 1660 Charles never went back to Scotland. An ancestor of the present Earl of Mansfield, Lord Stormont, was present at the Coronation.

Scone is magnificent but Falkland is a gem which will be enshrined in my heart for ever. The whole history of the unfortunate Stuarts is interwoven with that of the Palace. Here James V died after the Battle of Solway Moss, turning his face to the wall when the news was brought to him that his Queen, Mary of Guise, had given birth to a daughter at Linlithgow. He uttered the famous words, or prophecy, which came true. 'It cam' wi' a lass, it will gan' wi' a lass.' Walter the 6th Steward of Scotland married Marjory, daughter of Robert the Bruce, in 1315 and so brought the throne to his family, founding the

Royal House of Stewart. This form of spelling was used until the reign of Mary, Queen of Scots who changed the spelling in the French fashion to Stuart. Another lass, Queen Anne, was the last of her house to reign over Great Britain.

The baby born at Linlithgow grew up to be the tragic Mary of Scots, who spent much of her short reign hunting and hawking at Falkland. Here my beloved Charles II in 1651 presented new Colours to the Scottish troops who had been his bodyguard in Scotland. Thus the Scots Guards were formed. There is an exquisite model of the King stepping out of his coach to present the Colours to the assembled troops. It is quite impossible to describe the beauty of the gardens. I fell under a spell while walking through the peaceful policies with their gloriously coloured borders filled with roses, phlox, lavender, michaelmas daisies to name only a few. I have seen many famous gardens, yet none has left such a lasting impression as those at Falkland. (I hate ornamental gardens, too many are like municipal parks.) Here Mary Stuart must have walked during the short periods of happiness she enjoyed in her unruly kingdom. I cannot exonerate Mary entirely; she allowed her heart to rule her head, a privilege denied to royalty even today, and for a cultured woman Mary had the most deplorable taste in men. Perhaps her greatest tragedy was that she was too much a French-woman and too little a Scotswoman. Almost six feet tall with, as one historian describes, 'side long eyes', her most famous full length portrait is posthumous. Looking at her death mask, which is at Lennoxlove, it seems her beauty lay in the bone structure of her features. That she charmed men, even her jailers fell under her spell, there is no doubt. When I chugged my way in a motor boat to the island of Loch Leven where she was held prisoner I was trying to work out the relationship between Mary and her Douglas jailers. Lady Douglas had been a mistress of Mary's father, James V: therefore William Douglas, who dropped the napkin over the keys of the castle and so made her second escape possible, could have been her cousin! After all, the man who became Regent Moray was her half-brother! Illegitimate, of course. It was here at Loch Leven that Mary gave birth to still-born twins, the result of her brief

132

marriage with Bothwell, and here she was forced to sign the abdication in favour of her son by Darnley, the baby who became James VI of Scotland and James I of England. Mary's most fitting epitaph is the motto she embroidered as a girl, 'My beginning is my end'. It was by her manner of dying that she achieved immortality.

My publisher, and most of my long-suffering friends who will be press-ganged into proof reading for me, will be thankful that I have almost exhausted my memories. Everything I have written in this my final chapter has been written entirely from memory, without consulting any books of reference; if the result is somewhat incoherent so be it. I have made a resolve to plant rosemary in my garden; it seems appropriate and some of my close friends will understand why. Her Majesty Queen Elizabeth the Queen Mother is reputed to have remarked that 'Memories are the second happiness'. To a certain point I agree with Her Majesty, but memories can also rouse 'what might have been' and regrets for one's youth and lost opportunities. I have a poignant memory of walking down the Mound in 'Edinburgh Toon' so starry-eyed that an old woman gave me a sprig of white heather, and told me I had found my happiness. She was wrong.

O ye'll tak' the high road, and I'll tak' the low road,
And I'll be in Scotland afore ye,
But me and my true love will never meet again,
On the bonnie bonnie banks o' Loch Lomond.